The Haunted History of the Trans-Allegheny Lunatic Asylum

Sherri Brake

The Haunted History of the Trans-Allegheny Lunatic Asylum

Sherri Brake

Copyright © 2014 by Sherri Brake and Raven Rock
All rights reserved

Cover image by author

First published 2014

Printed in the United States

ISBN-13: 978-1466401198
ISBN-10: 1466401192

Library of Congress CIP data applied for.

Notice: The information in this book is true and complete to the best of our knowledge. It is offered without guarantee on the part of the author or Raven Rock. The author and Raven Rock disclaim all liability in connection with the use of this book.

All rights reserved. No part of this book may be reproduced or transmitted in any form whatsoever without prior written permission from the author except in the case of brief quotations embodied in critical articles and reviews.
To order signed copies of this book, contact the author at sherribrake@gmail.com

OTHER BOOKS BY THE AUTHOR

Haunted Stark County Ohio 2009
The Haunted History of the Ohio State Reformatory 2010
The Haunted History of the West Virginia Penitentiary 2011
Fireside Folklore of West Virginia Vol I 2102
Fireside Folklore of West Virginia Vol II 2014
Ghosthunters Guide to the West Virginia Pen 2014

WWW.HAUNTEDHISTORY.NET

Dedication

This book is dedicated to my
Aunt Lou (Green) Hammond.
Lou walked the halls of the asylum as a nurse
fresh out of nursing school. She experienced
sights and sounds in that building that remained with her for the rest
of her life. On occasion, she would share with us a story of her time
as a registered nurse at that facility.

This book is also dedicated to the asylum patient who insisted on
wearing a Superman cape in the halls, as he would try to fly.
Wherever you may be...

To the thousands of staff members,
We thank you for your service
during the history of the asylum.
To the patients who walked through the doors,
may you have found peace.

A special thank you to the Jordan family for preserving a piece of this nation's history.

CONTENTS

Chapter 1   My First Time..1
Chapter 2   The Devil Inside...6
Chapter 3   Kirkbride's Plan..15
Chapter 4   The Town in the Wilderness...........................28
Chapter 5   The Building of the Asylum............................34
Chapter 6   The Patients..44
Chapter 7   Drill the Skull and Ice the Body.......................56
Chapter 8   The Staff..71
Chapter 9   Reasons for Committal 78
Chapter 10   The White Plague Comes to Weston...............88
Chapter 11   Scandal, Fire, and Escape............................103
Chapter 12   The Closing..111
Chapter 13   Ghosts, Spirits and Shadows........................114
Chapter 14   Go Rest High on That Hill -the Cemeteries........138
Chapter 15   Various Photographs of the Asylum & Grounds..151
About the Author
Bibliography
Map

Weston Hospital 1989

Weston Hospital Treatment philosophy
The mission of Weston Hospital is to provide the most therapeutic treatment possible for those with mental illness in a humane environment respectful of individuality and dignity.

Official names of the asylum
1858-1863 Trans-Allegheny Lunatic Asylum
1863-1913 West Virginia Hospital for the Insane
1913-1980 Weston State Hospital
1980-1994 Weston Hospital
Also known as the Lunatic Asylum West of the Allegheny Mountains

1
My First Time

French Historian Alexis de Tocqueville once said, "When the past no longer illuminates the future, the spirit walks in darkness." He was a political thinker with his feet grounded firmly in the faith of Roman Catholicism. Alexis and I have nothing in common whatsoever, except that his famous quote popped into my head the very first time I laid eyes on a certain mammoth stone-cut building. I was in Weston, West Virginia.

The spirit walks in darkness, I thought. How apropos. As I gazed in awe at the largest stone cut building in the Western Hemisphere, I was glad I could leave this asylum of my own free will and not hear the doors slam shut as thousands of committed souls had done so in 150 years of operation.

The building had many names through the years of its operation: The West Virginia Hospital for the Insane, Weston State Hospital, Weston Hospital and the Trans Allegheny Lunatic Asylum. (TALA) When it first opened its doors in 1864, it was meant to house just 250 patients but by the 1950's, it was over crowded, under staffed, criticized for inhumane treatments and stained by scandals, patient murders, and suicides. The patient census climbed to 2400 people at the time the polio vaccine was created, DNA was discovered and Elvis was gyrating on the Ed Sullivan Show.

I could tell that time, the environment and neglect, had taken its toll on the building. Over a centuries worth of rain, snow and scorching summer sun had made its mark. Interior walls were crumbling and cracked and the paint was hanging from them looking like little daggers pointing downwards.

As I gazed at the vast expanse of beautiful green lawn sprawling around the asylum, the nice entrance road and welcoming water fountain in the round, I knew it would *not* be so welcoming once I walked inside those large front doors. I was right.

I had heard stories about this place growing up. You know when you are a kid and adults talk in hushed tones so you cannot make out what is being said? If you are like me, you probably tended to strain and try to hear the details not meant for your innocent ears. It was this way with some of the stories my Aunt Lou shared. I was raised in NE Ohio but with lots of family still back in central West Virginia. Aunt Lou was my mother's sister and what a sister she was! Always cracking jokes and telling stories. Aunt Lou was also the best registered nurse you could ever ask for and lived just a few miles from the hospital in the small town of Lost Creek. Her tales of working at Weston State Hospital were in instant recall the day I strolled through the big, heavy front door.

Trans-Allegheny Lunatic Asylum front drive 2008
Photo by author

The Haunted History of the Trans Allegheny Lunatic Asylum

It was a stifling summer day, the temperatures were in the 90s, and of course, of all days, this was the one day that I had chosen to do the long tour. I was in a group of about seven people and I was the only one with a camera, note pad and digital recorder. I must have looked like a reporter. The guide was very knowledgeable and had worked there at the same time my aunt had. She knew my aunt's name but could not recall anything else about her. I tried not to fall behind as we walked up and down the hallways, peering into small patient rooms with peeling paint and dirty bar covered windows, some of them broken like the dreams of many patients, I imagined. As I stood at one patient window in particular, I got instant goose bumps even though it was a muggy day both outside and inside the hospital. I acknowledged the fact that many patients locked inside this very room, had nothing else to do but stand in the same spot I was standing in and look at the same view I was seeing. It was creepy to say the least and I was glad the tour was starting again with a move on down the long and dim hallway. More than once, I saw some of the other tour guests glancing over their shoulders. You could almost feel it. The air was thick and stale but had a bit of a charge to it, for lack of a better word. It felt almost static-like as we climbed another staircase and made our way up to the doctor's quarters.

I was busy snapping photos and taking notes and wishing I had more than two hands. I was also wishing I had been more prepared in regards to possibly carrying a book bag. I had already bought a shirt and a book on Weston history from the gift shop. I was also glad I had left the high heels at home.

Photo by author 2008

As we climbed yet another staircase and stepped into one of the apartments, one of the women yelled suddenly and said someone had poked her in the middle of her back. The tour guide said simply "You'll have that sometimes." I knew exactly what she meant after owning a haunted tour company for over a decade, I was overly familiar with the paranormal as it was normal to. But for the woman who was poked in the back, it was anything *but* normal. I saw her dab her perspiring face with her sleeve repeatedly as her eyes darted to the corners of the room. She started to shuffle her feet a bit and seemed very nervous as she cleared her throat and asked if she could quit the tour early. Our tour guest was guided to a staircase and pointed the way down and out of the building. We waved goodbye and watched her leave our sight. The tour guide never said a word after that until we were downstairs at the end of our walk through. The guide said that she tried to keep her day tours strictly historic, but quite a few times someone would have an "experience" on her tour that defied explanation. This was one of those times.

The entrance to the Medical Center 2008
Photo by author

The long day tour continued without any more paranormal activity. We all enjoyed the historical information offered up and some of our guide's personal recollections of her working years at the hospital. We had explored all four floors of the main hospital building, had stepped inside the Medical building and had toured around the back of the hospital entering into a courtyard and another section of the hospital known as the Civil War section. This piqued my interest as I have been a Confederate Civil War re-enactor since 1998 and the 1860's had been my area of keen interest. The Civil War section is the oldest part of the hospital and I felt an immediate connection to it. Something told me that this area had to be pretty active, paranormally speaking, of course.

For the next 20 minutes, we continued with our tour and eventually maneuvered our way back to the main entrance area. It was still very hot and everyone (excluding me) was glad the tour was concluding. I could have walked and explored for hours!

We all thanked the matronly guide and several of us tipped her for her hospitality and tour knowledge. We said our goodbyes and ambled to the front door past an old timey wheelchair. The hot afternoon sun was shining thru the decorative glass transom windows above the front door. It was casting reflective glimmers of light and beautiful rainbows were dancing across the hospital floor. The historic day tour was over, but my love affair with an abandoned old asylum in West Virginia was just beginning.

2

The Devil Inside

I read the book *History of Psychiatry* many years ago while researching for haunted history tours at an old psychiatric hospital in Massillon, Ohio. I needed to brush up on my history of the treatment of the mentally ill and the evolution of certain treatments. As an American society, our views of dealing with those who are mentally challenged have evolved. Awareness of psychiatric disorders, medications and treatments has grown by leaps and bounds. We are far from perfect, but it's much better than the era of the 1770's when skull drilling was in fashion and Frenchman Philippe Pinel demanded "Unchain the Insane" in his crusade for better treatment of those with psychosis.

When I was in college in the 1981, I had an *Intro to Psychology* class at the University of Akron in Ohio. It started at 7am and I was usually still pretty groggy. Nothing would wake you up faster than viewing a film on transorbital lobotomies. During the first day of class we learned that Psychology is the study of the human mental processes and behavior. The term psychology comes from the Greek word "psyche" meaning "breath, spirit, soul" and the logia meaning the "study of." We studied the typical syllabus with introductions to the history of Psychiatry, and I learned Psychology studies both normal and abnormal behavior. When many people think about psychology, they immediately think about the diagnosis and treatment of abnormal behavior. However, it is important to remember that psychology studies normal behavior as well. We studied Pavlov, Jung and Freud and I found it all very fascinating. This was a lot of material to digest for a new college student but I loved it all. We touched briefly on psychiatric illness and spoke of "the manual". IO am referring to the *Diagnostic and Statistical Manual of Mental Disorders* that is used by clinicians and psychiatrists to diagnose psychiatric illnesses. Too bad something like this wasn't developed earlier, say back in the Medieval days when those deemed "mentally ill" were sometimes housed in cages or even worse.

The rapidly growing population of the United States during the 19th century, along with an ever-increasing number of immigrants, gave rise to the need for provision for the poor, the sick, and the mentally ill. Publicly supported almshouses and hospitals were established and the special needs of the mentally ill led to the era of asylums. The history of the treatment (or lack there of) of the mentally ill in the United States is a checkered one at best. The first colonists blamed mental illness on witchcraft and demonic possession, and the mentally ill were often imprisoned, sent to almshouses (also known as charitable house) or remained untreated at home. Conditions in these prison-like settings were appalling.

In many small towns in early America, it was not uncommon to have a 'village idiot' who wandered through the streets asking for handouts. This was not usually seen as a problem. On the occasion that they would become violent, they were often tolerated or would be put in the local jail as very few asylums operated in the United States before 1840. When the population grew across America, larger numbers of mentally unstable people would be found held in confinement. Unfortunately, their situation would gradually deteriorate.

The custody and care of the mentally ill were generally left to the individual's family early on in history, although some outside intervention occasionally occurred. Due to the shame and stigma attached to mental illness, many hid their mentally ill family members in cellars, caged them in pigpens, or put them under the control of house servants. Others were abandoned by their families and left to a life of begging, destitution and vagrancy. Surprisingly, the first mental hospital was established in Bagdad and built by the Muslims in 705 AD.

The first attempt to actually cure the mentally ill began in Great Britain and France with the rise of enlightenment in the 18th century. These new theories on treating mental illness (which spread to the United States by early 19th century) asserted that mental illness could be cured by removing the afflicted person from the environment. It was thought that by moving the person to the an institution of peace and quiet would be helpful. This explains why early institutions were recalled 'retreats' or 'asylums' as they were meant to be places of refuge and sanctuary.

In China, the mentally ill were hidden by their families for fear that the community would believe that the affliction was the result of immoral behavior and blamed on the individual and their relatives. The mentally ill were also thought to have 'bad fate' that would negatively influence anyone who associated with the disturbed individual. This would scare away potential suitors which could affect a future marriage. Many believed that mental illness was contagious and could be 'caught'.

Christians believed people were occasionally possessed by demonic forces, which needed to be ritually exorcised by priests. Some deeply embedded demons, often in elderly or eccentric women, could only be driven out by torture or death.

Our initial attempts to treat mental illness date back as early as 5000 BC. This was evidenced by the discovery of trephined skulls in regions that were home to world cultures and ancient civilizations. In ancient Mesopotamia, priest-doctors treated the mentally ill with magical-religious rituals, as mental pathology was believed to mask demonic possession. Exorcisms, incantations, prayer, atonement, and other various mystical rituals were used to drive out the evil spirit. Other means attempted to appeal to the spirit with more human devices; threats, bribery, punishment, and sometimes submission, were hoped to be an effective cure.

Ancient Hebrews believed that all illness was inflicted upon humans by God as an appropriate punishment for committing sin. It was even thought that demons could somehow bring about and cause mental illnesses and that these were attributed to God's wrath. Yet God was also seen as the ultimate healer and select Hebrew physicians were priests who had special ways of "appealing" to the higher power in order to cure mental disorders.

Through the Middle Ages and until the establishment of asylums, astrologers, witches, medical physicians, apothecaries and folk or traditional healers offered treatments for mental illness. Exorcisms, charms, amulets, prayers, roots, herbs, and various concoctions would be applied and used to help drive out the demons or cure the mind. The herb mugwort or St. John's Wort, would be worn in a charm on the body with Latin words of Mass or ritual worn around the neck. Sedatives would be used to help calm and tranquilize a violent patient. During the 17th century these consisted of opium, healing ointments or salves, and laudanum to help ease the torment of mental illness. Opium was also used dating back to 1500 BC, as a way to "stop a crying child". Heroin was given as a cure for the common cough as this vintage ad shows from Bayer Pharmaceutical.

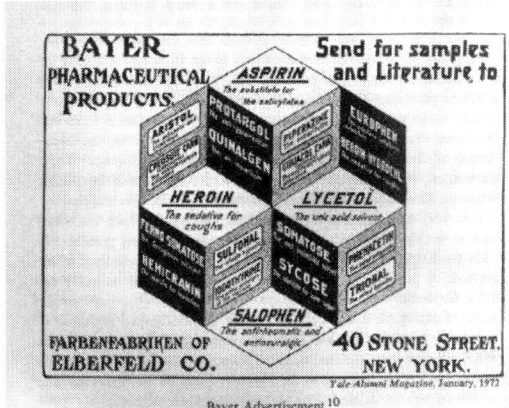

Bayer Advertisement [10]

Typical advertisement for cough relief with Heroin
From the authors collection

During the Middle Ages in Europe, mental illness was believed to result from an imbalance of bodily fluids such as phlegm, blood, yellow bile, and black bile. Hippocrates believed that existence was represented by the four basic elements; earth, air, fire, and water and in humans, this would be related to the four basic humors: blood, phlegm, black bile, yellow bile. These fluids, it was thought, produced the unique personalities of people and if these were imbalanced, then perhaps they could be balanced again and the person could be cured. How to accomplish this task? In order to bring the body back into its equilibrium state, patients were given laxatives emetics, and were bled using leeches. "Cupping" was also used which was a treatment in which heated cup-shaped vessels were applied to the skin in order to draw blood through the surface.

Bloodletting was practiced in the early days at Trans-Allegheny Lunatic Asylum. The first president of the United State, George Washington, fell prey to bloodletting. After riding in freezing weather, Washington developed a fever and went into respiratory distress. Under the care of his three physicians, he had vast amounts of blood drawn and laxatives were given. He died the next night with what has been diagnosed retrospectively as epiglottitis and shock. His medieval-type medical treatment aroused great controversy, particularly the bloodletting.

Priests and other clergy tried as best they could to help the 'demented' members of their flock. Private madhouses (as they were called) were established and run by members of the clergy to treat the mentally afflicted who could afford such expensive care. Countries following the Catholic faith regularly staffed mental health facilities with clergy, and most mentally ill individuals in Russia were housed in monasteries until asylums spread to the country in the mid-1800s.

In 1752, Quakers in Philadelphia were the first in America to make an organized effort to care for the mentally ill. The newly opened Pennsylvania Hospital provided rooms in the basement that were complete with shackles attached to the walls. Within a year or two, the need for more admissions required additional space, and a ward was opened adjacent to the hospital. Eventually, a new Pennsylvania Hospital for the Insane was built in a suburb in 1856 and remained open under different names until as late as 1998.

As the population of the country increased during the latter half of the 19th century and augmented by the entry of thousands of immigrants, the need for more beds in the asylums grew sharply. The early superintendents had fixed the size of the asylum to 250 beds so that the superintendent would actually recognize each patient. By 1866, they had raised the number of beds to 600. The early optimism about the curability of mental illness gave way as many patients proved to be in need of continuing care.

When ground broke for the building of the asylum in Weston in 1858, Benjamin Rush and Dorothea Dix had already taken the first step toward finding a treatment for the mentally ill by researching the causes.

Dorothea Dix

Benjamin Rush was one of the early founding fathers of the United States and hailed from the Philadelphia area. As a signer of the Declaration of Independence, Rush found himself in the company of Benjamin Franklin and John Hancock. Rush was a physician and a professor of chemistry, medical theory, and with clinical practice at the University of Pennsylvania. Rush argued that mental illness was the result of imbalances in the body's physical system and was caused by malfunctions in the brain. His approach prepared the way for later medical research and gained him the title, The Father of American Psychiatry. (He was also publishing the first textbook on the subject in the United States.) He was an avid proponent of bloodletting which was a practice used at TALA in the mid 19th century.

In the 1800s, patients in psychiatric wards had been the subject of cruelty, neglect and abuse. The staff was largely responsible for the majority of physical injury, sadly enough. Examples of the abuse are still debated, but here are some examples that most people would agree on today; female and male patients were subjected to take baths in ice-cold water, others were roped and led outside and forced to exercise like cattle. Some doctors would beat patients' heads into the wall to 'adjust' the body fluids and some were forced to sleep in tiny, unheated rooms. Some were even starved as "treatment".

Before 1844, the mentally ill were stashed away in the prisons and basements of public buildings. However, in the middle of the 19th century, reformers like Dorothea Dix pushed to improve the standing of those with serious mental illness. This led to an effort that spurred the construction of sprawling psychiatric hospitals with names like the State Lunatic Hospital at Danvers, Massachusetts and the Athens Lunatic Asylum in Athens, Ohio.

Dorothea Dix was born in 1802 in Hampden, Maine and for several decades, she worked to reform the situation and deplorable treatment of the indigent mentally ill in society. From 1843 to 1845, she investigated 18 state prisons, 500 almshouses and 300 county jails located across the United States. In 1841, she volunteered to teach a Sunday-school class for women prisoners as she was outraged by the conditions she witnessed.

Dorothea felt that the government had a moral obligation to care for certain people such as the insane, the blind, and the deaf. She believed that if a patient could recover from their illnesses, that they would be able to return to their position in society. This would cost the state much less money if their hospital stay were shortened. She also realized that some of the insane could be very dangerous to themselves, the local community and to their families. She believed that these patients needed treatment, confinement and understanding.

Confession is always weakness. The grave soul keeps its own secrets, and takes its own punishment in silence.----Dorothea Dix

Another woman made her mark on history as Dix had done. A New York Reporter, Nellie Bly, decided one day to disguise herself as a mentally ill person in order to view the treatment from a patient's point of view. It was in 1888, when journalist Nellie Bly, was approached by Joseph Pulitzer to write and expose about alleged rumors of the cruelty and neglect at the Blackwell's Island Insane Asylum in New York. . After Nellie rented a room at a local boardinghouse, she acted 'crazy' and was sent to the asylum shortly after enduring a quick examination. Bly put much thought into the situation beforehand. After a long night of practicing 'deranged' expressions in front of a mirror, she checked herself into a working-class boardinghouse. She refused to go to bed that night, telling the visitors that she was afraid of them and that they looked mad. They soon decided that *she* was crazy, and the next morning called the police. Nellie was taken to a courtroom where she pretended to have amnesia. The judge concluded she had possibly been drugged.

Nellie Bly

Nellie was examined by several doctors who all declared her insane. "Positively demented," said one, "I consider it a hopeless case. She needs to be put where someone will take care of her." Nellie found out after her committal, that hospitals had very poor conditions and that the food was usually old and stale. When Pulitzer finally sent a lawyer to Blackwell's, Nellie was released. She then began to write the true and disturbing story that exposed the dirtiness of the asylum. The public's reaction was complete outrage resulting in an increase of funding to several state asylums.

Her report was later published in book form as *Ten Days in a Mad-House*. This caused quite a sensation at the time and brought her great fame. She had tricked the establishment! While embarrassed physicians and staff fumbled to explain how so many working professionals had been fooled, a grand jury launched its own investigation into conditions at the asylum. They even invited Bly to assist. The jury's report recommended the changes she had proposed and its call for increased funds for care of the insane prompted an $850,000 increase in the budget of the Department of Public Charities and Corrections. They also made sure that future examinations were more thorough so that *only* the seriously ill actually went to the asylum.

I always had a desire to know asylum life more thoroughly - a desire to be convinced that the most helpless of God's creatures, the insane, were cared for kindly and properly.

Nellie Bly

Nellie Bly was quite a woman indeed. On a more pleasant note, she circled the globe with her travels completing the trip in seventy-two days just like the hero in Jules Verne's' *Around the World in 80 Days*. Nellie's life was cut short when she died of pneumonia at St. Mark's Hospital in New York City in 1922 at the age of fifty-seven. She had truly made her mark in the annals of journalism and psychiatry.

3
Kirkbride's Plan

The closing decade of the 19th century saw another shift in the care of mentally ill people. In response to the deteriorating conditions of the public hospitals, a number of physicians opened small, private asylums in their own homes for psychiatric patients. For the wealthy patient, hospitalization in a doctor's residence a "home away from home" was undoubtedly a welcome alternative to public care.

To some extent, the small private asylums resembled the early 19th-century hospitals promoted by two European reformers, Philippe Pinel (1745–1826) and William Tuke (1732–1822). Critical of the harsh treatment of the mentally ill in Europe at the time, Pinel and Tuke advocated using a regular routine and a pleasant environment—or moral therapy as it was called—as tools for treating mental illness. The large public hospitals were facing financial constraints and a growing patient population. They simply could not offer this type of attention to patients.

For the most part, private asylums offered the treatments that were popular at that time. In the late 19th and early 20th centuries, most physicians held a certain view of mental illness and assumed that a defect in the nervous system laid behind mental health problems. To correct the flawed nervous system, asylum doctors applied various treatments to patients' bodies, most often hydrotherapy, electrical stimulation and rest.

Enter Thomas Kirkbride. Thomas Story Kirkbride was born July 31st, 1809 to Quaker parents in rural Bucks County, Pennsylvania. His father was a descendent of Joseph Kirkbride of the Society of Friends, and hailed from the parish of Kirkbride, County of Cumberland, England. They came to America the same year that William Penn arrived. Penn was also a practicing Quaker. Kirkbride was often described as "humble, soft-spoken, simple and his dress, and reflective in his thoughts."

Dr. Kirkbride was a 1832 graduate of the medical department of the University of Pennsylvania. He was appointed as a resident physician of the Friends Asylum for the Insane at Frankford, and in March of 1833, he was elected resident physician of the Pennsylvania Hospital. He remained at the Pennsylvania Hospital for two years and had charge of the West Wing of the hospital in which the mentally 'insane' were treated.

Thomas Story Kirkbride

His ambition, intellect, and strong sense of purpose enabled him to use that position to become one of the most prominent authorities on mental health care in the latter half of the nineteenth century. In 1839, Kirkbride was elected a Fellow of the College of Physicians and retained his connection there until his death, which occurred forty-four years later. He was eventually invited to become Superintendent of the Mental Division of the Pennsylvania Hospital, which had gradually increased in size since its establishment. In October of 1840 and with the new hospital structure approaching completion, Kirkbride was elected physician. At that time, there were only around ten hospitals for the insane scattered throughout the United States. Though the proper principles that help to regulate the care and the treatment of the mentally ill were not quite recognized or understood yet, Kirkbride and his theories were well received.

In regards to Kirkbride's opinion on some of the archaic treatments for psychiatric ailments, he eventually announced the discontinuing of bloodletting and other so-called depleting measures of treatment. He insisted that the buildings that housed the insane be called 'hospitals'. He believed that the patients and their recovery would be greatly influenced by the environment and that if the wards were made more attractive and the grounds beautified by trees, shrubs, and flowers, that the mentally ill would recover more quickly and be able to be released into society much sooner.

Dr. Kirkbride was a strong advocate of "moral treatment," a philosophy based upon compassion and respect for the insane. He sought to create a humane environment where both rich and poor were treated with dignity. He believed patients responded to greater freedom with better behavior. Persons suffering from insanity, he insisted, "Are not disabled from appreciating books...or enjoying many intellectual and physical comforts." While only half of Dr. Kirkbride's patients eventually recovered and resumed their positions in the world, this remains a striking accomplishment in an era when effective medications and other modern treatments were virtually non-existent.

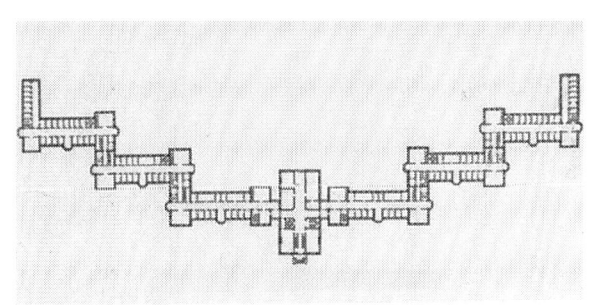

Typical Kirkbride building design

When the hospital in Philadelphia was proposed, Kirkbride provided the layout for the construction. His hospital plan was linear with a central building to house administrative offices, kitchens and staff living quarters with wings extending on either side. Each ward had a wide central corridor with sitting alcoves, single patient rooms, and small dormitories. Multiple wards allowed for classification of patients according to their condition. Kirkbride paid much attention to details such as ventilation, heating, sanitary arrangements, and space for patient occupation and recreation.

> "THERE IS NO REASON WHY AN INDIVIDUAL WHO HAS THE MISFORTUNE TO BECOME INSANE, SHOULD, ON THAT ACCOUNT, BE DEPRIVED OF ANY COMFORT OR EVEN LUXURY..."
>
> THOMAS KIRKBRIDE

Dr. Kirkbride also appreciated the importance of training nurses and attendants to perform the duties not of a *keeper* but as loyal and sympathetic caretakers or attendants. In his report for 1845 he stated "I propose to give to those employed in this institution, as my engagements per minute, of regular course of instruction on the nature of their duties-embracing some general views of the character and peculiarities of the diseases which are affecting our patients-the principles which should regulate their intercourse with them and with each other-the proper mode of proceeding in different cases, and such other matters as would be likely to give them a just sense of the importance and responsibility of their calling."

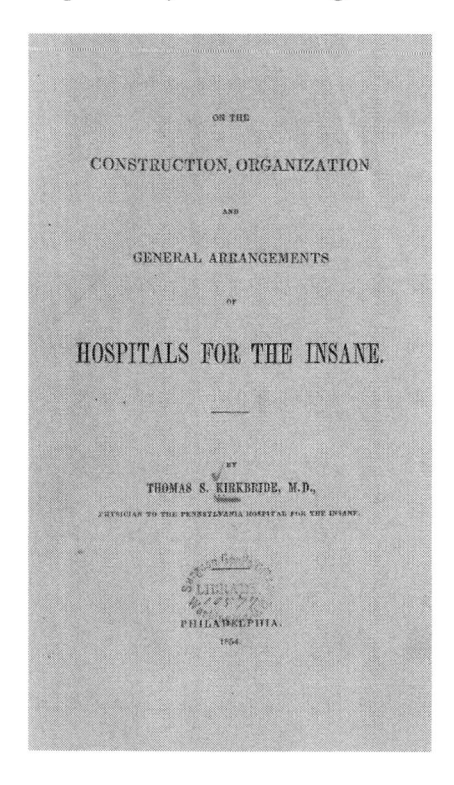

ON THE

CONSTRUCTION, ORGANIZATION

AND

GENERAL ARRANGEMENTS

OF

HOSPITALS FOR THE INSANE.

BY

THOMAS S. KIRKBRIDE, M.D.,

PHYSICIAN TO THE PENNSYLVANIA HOSPITAL FOR THE INSANE.

PHILADELPHIA.
1854.

In 1854, Thomas Story Kirkbride published his widely read book, "On the Construction, Organization and General Arrangements of Hospitals for the Insane." If you have ever done any research on historical asylums, you have probably heard of the term 'Kirkbride Building'. This book was used as the blueprint on how to correctly construct and arrange hospitals for the mentally ill during the nineteenth century. Dr. Kirkbride was a visionary leader in the early, formative years of psychiatry who advocated for moral treatment. This was the belief that patients should be treated with kindness and sympathetic care. He encouraged the use of the term 'hospital' and discouraged the use of the terms 'asylum' and 'lunatic'. New York State did not adopt the term 'hospital' for all of their asylums for the insane until 1890. This was thirty-six years after the book was published. Dr. Kirkbride also recommended that hospitals for the insane should not exceed 250 patients, which, as we all know, were not followed for very long.

At a meeting of "The Association of Medical Superintendents of American Institutions for the Insane," held at Philadelphia, in May 1851, the following series of propositions relative to the construction of *Hospitals for the Insane* was unanimously adopted. The succeeding series of propositions for institutions was also adopted:

Propositions Relative to the Construction of Hospitals for the Insane.

I. Every hospital for the insane should be in the country, not within less than two miles of a large town, and easily accessible at all seasons.

II. No hospital for the insane, however limited its capacity, should have less than fifty acres of land, devoted to gardens and pleasure grounds for its patients. At least one hundred acres should be possessed by every State hospital, or other institution for two hundred patients, to which number these propositions apply, unless otherwise mentioned.

III. Means should be provided to raise ten thousand gallons of water, daily, to reservoirs that will supply the highest parts of the building.

IV. No hospital for the insane should be built without the plan having been first submitted to some physician or physicians who have had charge of a similar establishment, or are practically acquainted with all the details of their arrangements, and received his or their full approbation.

V. The highest number that can with propriety be treated in one building is two hundred and fifty, while two hundred patients is a preferable maximum.

VI. All such buildings should be constructed of stone or brick, have slate or metallic roofs, and, as far as possible, be made secure from accidents by fire.

VII. Every hospital, having provision for two hundred or more patients, should have in it at least eight distinct wards for each sex, making sixteen classes in the entire establishment.

VIII. Each ward should have in it a parlor, a corridor, single lodging-rooms for patients, an associated dormitory, communicating with a chamber for two attendants; a clothes-room, a bath-room, a water-closet, a dining-room, a dumb-waiter, and a speaking-tube leading to the kitchen or other central part of the building.

IX. No apartments should ever be provided for the confinement of patients, or as their lodging-rooms, that are not entirely above ground.

X. No class of rooms should ever be constructed without some kind of window in each, communicating directly with the external atmosphere.

XI. No chamber for the use of a single patient should ever be less than eight by ten feet, nor should the ceiling of any story occupied by patients be less than twelve feet in height.

XII. The floors of patients' apartments should always be of wood.

XIII. The stairways should always be of iron, stone, or other indestructible material, ample in size and number, and easy of ascent, to afford convenient egress in case of accident from fire.

XIV. A large hospital should consist of a main central building with wings.

XV. The main central building should contain the offices, receiving rooms for company, and apartments, entirely private, for the superintending physician and his family, in case that officer resides in the hospital building.

XVI. The wings should be so arranged that, if rooms are placed on both sides of a corridor, the corridors should be furnished at both ends with movable glazed sashes, for the free admission of both light and air.

XVII. The lighting should be by gas, on account of its convenience, cleanliness, safety, and economy.

XVIII. The apartments for washing clothing should be detached from the hospital building.

XIX. The drainage should be under ground, and all the inlets to the sewers should be properly secured to prevent offensive emanations.

XX. All hospitals should be warmed by passing an abundance of pure, fresh air from the external atmosphere, over pipes or plates, containing steam under low pressure, or hot water, the temperature of which at the boiler does not exceed 212° F., and placed in the basement or cellar of the building to be heated.

XXI. A complete system of forced ventilation, in connection with the heating, is indispensable to give purity to the air of a hospital for the insane; and no expense that is required to effect this object thoroughly can be deemed either misplaced or injudicious.

XXII. The boilers for generating steam for warming the building should be in a detached structure, connected with which may be the engine for pumping water, driving the washing apparatus, and other machinery.

XXIII. All water-closets should, as far as possible, be made of indestructible materials, be simple in their arrangements, and have a strong downward ventilation connected with them.

XXIV. The floors of bath-rooms, water-closets, and basement stories, should, as far as possible, be made of materials that will not absorb moisture.

XXV. The wards for the most excited class should be constructed with rooms on but one side of a corridor, not less than ten feet wide, the external windows of which should be large, and have pleasant views from them.

XXVI. Wherever practicable, the pleasure-grounds of a hospital for the insane, should be surrounded by a substantial wall, so placed as not to be unpleasantly visible from the building."

Souce: "On The Construction, Organization and General Arrangements of Hospitals For The Insane" by Thomas S. Kirkbride, M.D., Physician to the Pennsylvania

Hospital for the Insane, Philadelphia, 1854, Pages 72-78.

In 1851, the Superintendents' Association adopted 26 propositions written by Kirkbride for hospital design which served as official policy for 40 years, and Kirkbride served as President of the Association from 1862 to 1870. After 1870, as the average hospital size increased (to over 10,000 beds in the 20th century), Kirkbride's influence declined. In 1888, the Association voted to "not affirm" Kirkbride's propositions. When Kirkbrides plan for the new Trans Allegheny Lunatic Asylum was presented, it most surely met this requirement of the Kirkbride Plan

> *"The building should be in a healthful, pleasant and fertile district of country; the land chosen should be of good quality and easily tilled; the surrounding scenery should be of a varied and attractive kind, and the neighborhood should possess numerous objects of an agreeable and interesting character. While the hospital itself should be retired and its privacy fully secured, it is desirable that the views from it should exhibit life in its active forms, and on this account stirring objects at a little distance are desirable. Reference should also be made to the amount of wood and tillable land that may be obtained, to the supply of water, and to the facilities for drainage, and for enclosing the pleasure grounds."*

One only needs to look at the current footprint of the main hospital building get a sense of the peacefulness of the area. The gently rolling hills behind the building, the grassy expanse of front lawn and the West Fork River to its front. A perfect idyllic setting for an asylum, if there is such a thing. The article goes on to state:

> *"Amount of Land.—Every hospital for the insane should possess at least one hundred acres of land, to enable it to have the proper amount for farming and gardening purposes, to give the desired degree of privacy and to secure adequate and appropriate means of exercise, labor and occupation to the patients, for all these are now recognized as among the most valuable means of treatment. Of the total amount, from thirty to fifty acres immediately around the building-?, should be appropriated as pleasure grounds, and should be so arranged and enclosed as to give the patients the full benefit of them, without being annoyed by the presence of visitors or others. It is desirable that several acres of this tract should be in groves or woodland, to furnish shade in Summer, and its general character should be such as will admit of tasteful and agreeable, improvements.*

While reading thru "On the Construction, Organization, and General Arrangements of Hospitals for the Insane" book by Mr. Kirkbride, one can get a true feel for how compassionate and truly caring he was.

My only motive is to be useful to the insane, and the community, to save Boards of Trustees or Managers, the trouble and disappointment of resorting to experiments, which have been tried over and over again, and always with bad results, and to enable those who take charge of new Hospitals, to begin under circumstances that will allow them, from the start, to devote themselves to the welfare of their patients, and thus show the public how much good these institutions are capable of effecting.

Kirkbride even offers up suggestions for salaries for hospital employees in 1854 at the time of the publishing of his book.

Schedule of a Complete Organization with Rate of Compensation.—The following list, as before remarked, is believed to include only those that are necessary about a State Hospital for the Insane, when containing 250 patients, and that is to be managed efficiently,

A Board of Trustees,..........................Expenses to be paid.
A Treasurer, non-resident,..................Salary, $250 per annum.
One Physician-in-Chief,.......................$1,500 per annum,
with furnished apartments and board of family.
If living detached and finding his family,.........$1,000 additional.
One First Assistant Physician,...........Board and $500 per annum.
One Second Assistant Physician,.......... $300
One Steward,........................ $500
One Matron,......................... $300
One Male Supervisor,................ $250
One Female Supervisor,............. $175
One Male Teacher,................... "
One Female Teacher,................. "
Sixteen Male Attendants,.............$168
Sixteen Female Attendants,..........$108
One Night Watchman,..................$168
One Night Watchwoman,............ $108
Two Seamstresses,..........................$96

One Farmer,	*$200*
Two Farm hands,	*$144*
One Gardener,	*$200*
One Assistant Gardener,	*$144*
One Engineer,	*$240*
Two Firemen,	*$144*
One Baker,	*$150*
One Carpenter,	*$240*
One Carriage Driver,	*$168*
One Jobber,	*$144*
One Cook,	*$150*
Two Assistant Cooks,	*$100*
Four Female Domestics,	*$80*
One Dairy Maid,	*$100*
Three Washerwomen,	*$100*
Three Ironers,	*$100*

As far as Kirkbride's suggestions on the treatment and housing of the more violent and law breaking patients, he offers this;

> *There is a certain class of old offenders and notorious prison-breakers, as well as dangerous homicides, who, whether sane or insane, should never be allowed to have a greater degree of liberty than can be found within the walls of a well constructed prison. Hard as this opinion may seem to bear on a few individuals, who have already taken or attempted to take life, or have deeply outraged the laws and the peace of society, still it is as nothing in comparison to the cruelty and injustice that would be done to a whole community, who had never committed an offence, by exposing them to the risks which must always attend the enlargement of such dangerous men, even during a lucid interval. There are many of this class who can never be safely at large, nor yet be kept securely in any hospital properly arranged for the treatment of the insane, without converting a part of it into a prison, or exposing the other patients to risks which no plea of that kind of morbid benevolence, which seems to regard with much greater sympathy the fate of a condemned felon than the sufferings of his innocent victims and their families, can ever justify. There are other cases, however, who occasionally get to prison wrongfully, persons who are not especially dangerous in their propensities, but who, while in a state of irresponsibility, have committed acts contrary to the laws, and who ought originally to have been sent to*

a hospital for treatment, instead of to a prison for punishment. Certain cases of insanity, too, that originate in prison may safely be transferred to a hospital for treatment, provided it is deemed expedient to remove convicts at all who become insane after entering a prison, and thus in a measure relieving them from the penalties of their sentence. If many of this class are received into any ordinary hospital for the insane, it can hardly be questioned but that the popular sentiment will be strongly aroused against the measure, especially as escapes will be of such frequent occurrence as to keep the neighborhood in a state of alarm, unless apartments entirely distinct from those of the other patients and of a different character are provided.

The Kirkbride plan called for the more quiet and better controlled patients to be close to the center or core of the hospital floor plan. This was to insure a more unobtrusive zone for visitors and staff. The louder and more violent patients would have rooms farthest away from the center of the building.

It will be found desirable, in practice, that the least excited—what is commonly called the best class of patients—should occupy the upper stories and be nearest the centre building, while the noisy should be at a distance, and the feeble in the lower story; but it is impossible to give any general rule that will be satisfactory in all respects to a novice in the management of the insane. The best arrangement, after all, will be to associate in the same ward those who are least likely to injure and most likely to benefit each other, no matter what may be the character or form of their disease, or whether supposed to be curable or incurable. No one, of course, would think of placing the violent and the calm, the noisy and the quiet, nor the neat and the filthy, together; but there are many grades between most of these, and individuals of extremely different character, who, nevertheless, do well together. Variety is as pleasant to a hospital patient as to anyone else, and even if it were practicable, it is not probable that it would be found satisfactory to have all our associates exactly like ourselves. Patients are often much interested in the delusions of their neighbors, and by their efforts to relieve the afflictions of others, frequently do much towards getting rid of their own.
Restraint and Seclusion.—The use of mechanical means of restraint, and the protracted seclusion of patients in their rooms—although the firmer of them maybe, and, as I believe, is occasionally desirable, but not absolutely necessary, in the management of our Hospitals for the In-

sane—ought both always to be regarded as evils of no trifling magnitude, and to abate which, as far as possible, no effort should be left untried. They both tend to produce a relaxation of vigilance, and it cannot be too often repeated, that whatever tends to make vigilance unnecessary is undesirable about a Hospital for the Insane. Besides leading patients into bad habits, the frequent use of the means referred to, in a ward, induces attendants and others to look upon them as a common resource in cases of difficulty or danger, to regard them as their grand reliance in every emergency, and to forget the great power of other measures that are entirely unobjectionable—the value of tact and kindness and sympathy in controlling the violence and dangerous propensities of the insane. And yet, without a proper force of attendants and an efficient classification, the use of mechanical means of restraint and the protracted seclusion of certain classes of patients is almost unavoidable.

Objectionable as I deem the use of restraining apparatus in a Hospital for the Insane, it cannot be too earnestly insisted on, that it is no advance to give up mechanical means of restraint and to substitute the frequent and long-continued seclusion of the patients. Occasionally an individual may really be more comfortable and much better off in the open air, with some mild kind of restraining apparatus on his person, than he would be confined to his room without it; for this kind of long-continued seclusion is pretty sure, sooner or later, to lead to habits revolting in themselves and most unfortunate for the future prospects of the patient.

Thomas Kirkbride's ideas brought about mixed feelings in both patients and peers. Some in the medical community saw his theories and ideas as stubbornly clinging to ideals that hindered medical progress, while others supported his ideas, and saw them change the treatment philosophy for the mentally insane. In his patients, he sometimes inspired fear and anger, even to the point that one attempted to murder him, but he also believed that the mentally ill could be treated, and possibly cured. Dr. Kirkbride had his own practice from 1835 to 1840. He pioneered what would be known as the Kirkbride Plan to improve medical care for the mentally ill by using a standardized building plan to house the patients. He died December 16, 1883 in Philadelphia, Pennsylvania at the age of seventy-four after complications from pneumonia. It was known that Kirkbride's ideas brought about various mixed feelings during his lifetime. Both patients, his peers and the medical community occasionally believed that his plans hindered medical progress, while others saw his ideas as groundbreaking.

The Kirkbride building plan was implemented in the design of various hospitals including the Athens Lunatic Asylum in Ohio, Buffalo State Hospital in New York and Danvers State Hospital in Danvers Massachusetts. Other examples include St. Elizabeth Hospital in Washington DC, Traverse City Hospital in Michigan and of course, Trans-Allegheny Lunatic Asylum.

In the latter half of the 20th century, the invention of anti-psychotic drugs such as Thorazine triggered a movement toward "Deinstitutionalization" so much so that by the year 2000 almost all of the Kirkbride buildings had been abandoned or downsized. The shells of the grand structures, and tales of the horrors they housed, still remain.

4
The Town in the Wilderness

Millions of years ago, central West Virginia was situated in the bed of a great sea which scientists named the Appalachian Sea. The actual bottom of the sea was around 10,000 feet below the present level of the valley at Weston. There were tiny animals like corals, which lived on the bottom of the sea floor and their hard shells became built up layer by layer, until the deposit was several feet in thickness. The sea eventually became filled up until it was nothing but a swamp where ferns grew as well as other plants and eventually many layers of silt were deposited upon it. The lush ferns grew and flourished for many years. Rivers and creeks flowed through the new forests that eventually sprouted. Native American Indians were able to live and thrive without any the comforts of civilization until the hardworking and sturdy race of Virginia woodsman and pioneers battled their way in, clearing timber and settling the area with their cabins and improvements.

According to Indian tradition, the Iroquois in the year 1713 'leased' the rights to hunt and fish in the area now known as the Mountain State. The Iroquois allowed the Shawnee and the Delaware to visit this area. The Shawnee often came in large groups as well, they would bring their women, and children with them, sometimes remaining from early fall until the approach of the harsh mountain winters. They would then return to their villages towards the north and in Ohio. The Indians often came to Hackers Creek for their hunting ground and two others farther east by way of trails leading up the little Kanawha River from its mouth and then across the divide to the waters of the West Fork. The West Fork River would soon become a source of sandstone for the building of the Trans Allegheny Lunatic Asylum.

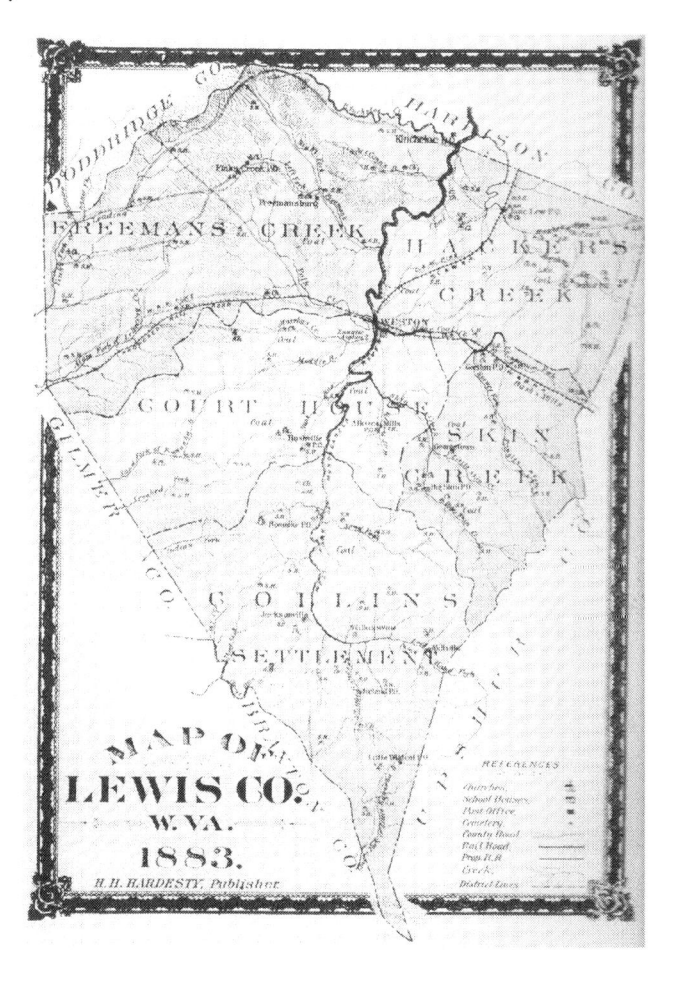

According to some sources of folklore and history, the Shawnee would not locate villages in the area now known as West Virginia because they believed the area to have a dark and negative energy. Native American Indians tended to avoid what is now West Virginia because they viewed it as a mysterious place plagued by vengeful ghosts and mysterious monsters as the lands that fell between the Ohio River from the Potomac River were often filled with dreadful stories shared among the tribes.

It is documented that the first permanent settler in what is now Lewis County was a man by the name of John Hacker. He had made his claim and had cleared part of his land. Hacker built his cabin in the fall of 1769. These early pioneers of Western Virginia were a hardy bunch as many were Scots Irish immigrants.

The end of the Indian Wars occurred after the Treaty of Paris was signed in 1783.Unfortunatley that treaty that did not actually bring peace with the Indians for 12 years longer the settlements on the western border were subjected the sudden attacks and raids. The Trans Allegheny settlers were very disappointed in their expectations of a civilized settlement until many more years passed.

With the encroaching of settlers, a log courthouse was constructed in Lewis County and was used as a meeting place. Crime was easily found on the frontier as evidenced from this sampling of courthouse records from 1785. Several of these citations would have been proof enough of assignment to the Asylum if it had been constructed at this time!

1785 Grand Jury Presentments:

Daniel Fink for Drunkenness and disorderly behavior

John Wolf for getting drunk

Thomas Nuttier for getting drunk

Peter Kinchelo for being drunk, swearing and being disorderly

James McDead and James Meeks for assault and battery on evidence of Obediah Davisson

Samuel Harker for breach of the Sabbath Day on the evidence of Mary Cutrack

Robert Pike for theft on the evidence of Caleb Stout

Benjamin Coplin, Evan Thomas and Daniel Fink for allowing card playing in their Houses to the knowledge of two of the jurymen.

Samuel Burris for getting drunk

M. McCann for keeping a tipling house to the disorder of the public on Gilbert

Hustage and Major Power's evidence

James Goof and Mary Anderson for living in adultery to the knowledge of two of the jurymen

Jonathan Crouch and Catherine Riffle for living in adultery to the knowledge of two of the jurymen

Wm. Angling for living in adultery with a certain woman

Benjamin Coplin for allowing card playing last evening by David Murphy and Josiah Davisson, Jr., Charles Harris and John Webb

Charles Harris for getting drunk

After the battle of Fallen Timbers, the Native American Indians were unable to withstand the rush of the first line of the white settlers. By the Treaty of Greenville in 1795, they agreed to give up their lands in what is now Ohio, with the exception of the strip in the northern part of the state. It appeared that the settlements, which had been maintained in the Lewis County area, would be at last free to expand without fear of further massacres or invasions. As the Indians began to retreat farther westward, civilization encroached one cabin at a time.

The first settlor into the Weston area was Revolutionary War Veteran, Henry Flesher. He built his cabin and established his farm in 1818. His farmland would eventually be selected by the commissioners as the County seat of Lewis County and the site for the new town. The town was laid out by Colonel Edward Jackson who was grandfather to Civil War General Thomas Jonathan "Stonewall" Jackson. Jackson was employed to lay off the town into lots and to mark the streets accordingly. The lots were then sold off to prospective homebuilders and merchants,

Building operations began at once and a small village began to emerge with a total of ten to fifteen log houses. There was only one frame building in the town at that time which stood opposite the courthouse. In January 1818, the General Assembly passed an act that established the town as the new town of Preston. A problem soon arose as it was thought the town of Preston would be confused with Preston County, which was in Virginia. Many of the citizens of the town objected strongly to the new name. Henry Flesher, after selling a part of his farm on the east side of the river, had moved to the other side and had built his cabin upon what is now part of the Trans-Allegheny Lunatic Asylum lawn. He consistently and stubbornly refused to have anything to do with the development of the town. His objections were so strong that some of the influential citizens in town secured a bill changing the name of the town. This time it bore the name of Weston. The year was 1819.

The development of the town of Weston was rapid. Churches were built along with schools, a gristmill, hotels, stores, a wagon shop, a gunsmith shop, a farm equipment store, and other buildings. Theaters were eventually built in town but not until after the end of the Civil War.

The founding of Weston had considerable amount of influence in the development of the surrounding land. This was partly due to the fact that most of the townspeople bought small farms in the vicinity. It was from these farms that they obtained their firewood and raised their crops. Very few of the farmers owned slaves because they could not afford to keep them. Only the very rich farmers could afford to keep slaves and many were used for domestic service as well as in the field.

Some would call this frontier justice while others would simply call it a lynching. Nonetheless, Edgar Jones died by hanging as his body can be seen here dangling under the bridge across the West Fork. The outline of the asylum can be seen in the distance. July 6th 1892

With the developing of the town and outlying areas, a regular stagecoach line was established between Weston and Staunton. The Staunton and Parkersburg turnpike was one of the causes of great business prosperity at the time. This route connected the county seat with points north and south and brought business and immigration into the area more readily. With the continuing development of the town of Weston came a great opportunity in 1858. With the growth of population west of the Alleghenies and inadequacy of the few existing asylums, the General Assembly decided to establish a new institution. The Assembly had chosen three possible sites for the building of such an institution: Fayetteville in Fayette County, Sutton in Braxton County and Weston in Lewis County. Weston was now in the running for Virginia's third mental hospital. The winds of change were rapidly approaching.

5
The Building of the Asylum

The construction of the largest hand cut stone building in North America began in 1858 but was eventually stalled by the outbreak of the Civil War and 1861 the asylum was originally opened as the West Virginia hospital for the insane soon after West Virginia became a state in 1863.

The first patients arrived in 1864 but construction of the building was not completed until 1881. The building was constructed primarily of blue sandstone was surrounded by large trees. It was enclosed by a seemingly unending line of black wrought iron fence. The architect for the building was Richard Snowden Andrews.

Andrews was born in October of 1830 in Baltimore, Maryland. He was not only an architect, but was also an artillery commander during the War Between the States. He had organized the First Maryland Light Artillery and was wounded at the First Days Battle in July of 1862. After the war, he designed the Maryland governor's residence in Annapolis and the south wing of the United State treasury building in Washington DC. Andrews passed away on January 5, 1903 with his greatest accomplishment standing second in size to the Kremlin.

The main hospital building stands resilient today and not far from the banks of the West Fork River in central West Virginia. Back before the building of the Trans-Allegheny Lunatic Asylum commenced there were only two other mental institutions in the state of Virginia. These were located at Staunton and Williamsburg. This new institution was to be built in the western portion of the state, which would be west of the Alleghenies, and it was this location that factored into the naming of the facility.

Vintage postcard, author's collection

Several important Weston citizens had government positions in Richmond Virginia at this time Jonathan M. Bennett who was the first auditor of Virginia, Sen. John Brannon and delegate William Arnold. They all lobbied heavily for the state hospital. Before the arrival of the selection committee in town, this group encouraged that the town of Weston prepare fences were to be amended sidewalks repaired houses were to be washed and painted trash was to be hauled away, and holes in the streets were to be filled or graveled. The entire town needed to appear prosperous and gregarious. When the building commissioners arrived, they were greeted with much pomp and circumstance with the band playing and a group of children leading the parade to the proposed building site.

There was much talk and debate over Weston as a choice for the hospital site. Though Weston was small and did not have a railroad, it did have easily accessible coal, water, stone, and timber to use as ongoing resources for any building that might be erected. Supporters declared that the town's lack of railroad access was an asset, since Weston was a little more isolated from the hustle and bustle of modern life. This could really be construed as a plus since many authorities at that time, believed the strain and stress of modern life led to increased insanity and possible hysteria for women.

The celebrated commissioners were wined, dined and entertained for the week that they were present. They evaluated the site along the river and were wise to note the amount of water and generous amount of stone and timber for use of building materials. Bennett, Brannon, and Arnold reaped the benefits of their resourcefulness and having the town whitewashed. The commissioners unanimously decided that the new state mental institution would be located in Weston.

The choosing of the town as the location of the new state asylum was probably one of the most important events in the history of the town of Weston. It was hoped that new families would move in and build homes, stores would prosper with the sale to laborers and new townspeople and the population of the area would increase naturally. There had been about four hundred people in Weston and 1855 and the population would more than double within ten years.

There was much to do. The Board had purchased 269 acres of land at $36.47 an acre for a total of $9,809.12. Second, the Board hired Francis T. Striblin and Dr. Thomas Kirkbride as advisors in the building plan, and employed Andrews as architect. They used the Kirkbride Plan, which had already been used on many other hospitals in the 1800s. The building was planned to cost $253,000, which was a number they realized later was excessively small.

Vintage postcard from the author's collection

Construction started in 1858, with Mr. Goulding from Baltimore chosen to be the topographical engineer, and German born John McGee, to be the superintendent. First, the grounds were cleaned and prepared for the building. Prisoners, and seven "Negro convicts," were forced to complete this task, collect rocks from the quarry, and make them into bricks. One of the first buildings completed on the grounds was for these workers to live in. Two other buildings were constructed with those being a sawmill and a brick making building with ovens. Because of these two buildings, all the materials for the hospital were made on site.

SAID TO BE DANGEROUS
5 Of 9 Weston Escapees Loose

By TOM SAWYER
Of The Daily Mail Staff

Five of nine inmates who escaped from the security ward at Weston State Hospital early today remained at large this afternoon.

They were the object of a widespread search by police throughout the state who have set up roadblocks and watches.

All five are described by police as dangerous. Two are transfers from the State Penitentiary.

In escaping from the hospital, the inmates overpowered hospital aide James Webber, 53, and knifed him. He was treated at Stonewall Jackson Hospital at Weston for an arm wound. The five at large were identified by the Department of Mental Health as:

Rice Lafferty, 27, of Scarbro, Fayette County; Stonewall Jackson Davis, 59, of Sutton; Frankin D. Haney of Paintsville, Ky.; Curtis Oliver Rensforth, 35, of Elm Grove, and Eugene Blake, 22, of Wayne.

Late this morning, police picked up William Sheridan Poe, 18, of Morgantown. He was apprehended in the Weston area.

Charleston Daily Mail August 29ʰ 1867

The building of the asylum caused great interest across the state, especially when news came of the asylum break out. The local newspaper noted, "Seven Convict Negroes" as the first workers and similarly the first to escape. There were twenty-three men sent by Governor. Wise from Richmond to begin work. One would wonder how they accomplished the act. They seemingly convinced their guards that they had "urgent necessities outside the prison." As this was a rain filled gloomy night, chaos soon ensued. The escapees apparently did not know the area very well as they were all eventually recaptured within a few days and not far away in distance. Hospital history mentions that they were thereafter "kept under a stricter watch." A blockhouse for these men was one of the first buildings built up on the hospital grounds.

Highly skilled stonemasons arrived later from Ireland and Germany. Workers were hired and convict labor was utilized with the making of bricks and the quarrying of stone. The sandstone was easily tooled with the chisel and hammer and was initially quarried in nearby Harrison County. It was then hauled back to the hospital site by horse and wagon, at great cost. A budget cutting decision was made when a new supply of sandstone was 'discovered' on the bank of the West Fork River just about 600 feet from the hospitals main building. This enabled a single mule to haul the blocks from the neighboring river instead of hauling from over the hill and in the neighboring county.

The design of the Weston hospital would follow the typical pattern of Kirkbride buildings with a central structure being approximately four stories high and sitting in the center. From this center section, long straight wings would extend off like long arms. Many of the Kirkbride buildings have tall cupolas as an architectural detail. The designers of these institutions always tried to maintain a proper and fixed order with repetitious lines to bring about order in the lives of the mentally ill. Abundant light and air were mandatory in the Kirkbride plan it was to help improve health of the residents as well improve the morale of the staff.

The building of asylum was underway until the spring of 1861 arrived and the eruption of the War Between the States exploded across the nation....and in the town of Weston. Virginia had seceded from the union but many in the western portion of the state would choose to remain loyal to the Union and the North. The construction of the asylum was stopped by an order the government of Virginia and it was announced that the collected money in the sum of $27,000 be returned to Richmond to help with the defending of the state and the war. Who would guess that this money would eventually end up playing an important part in helping to establish the brand-new government of the newly formed state of West Virginia?

Presley Hale was a young unionist storekeeper from Weston who suggested to the new governor Francis Pierpont, that the money in the bank in Weston be used before the Confederate government and Richmond gained control of it. Pierpont sent Presley Hale to meet with Union General George McClellan in Grafton. McClellan then ordered the Seventh Ohio Infantry, who had just arrived in Clarksburg by train, to immediately travel to Weston. McClellan then sent an urgent message to the Colonel of the Seventh Ohio Infantry, which read, "Get your troops to Weston, Lewis County, at once. Confiscate all the gold in the Weston bank, by force if necessary. Ship it to Gov. Pierpont at Wheeling, hurray for New Virginia!"

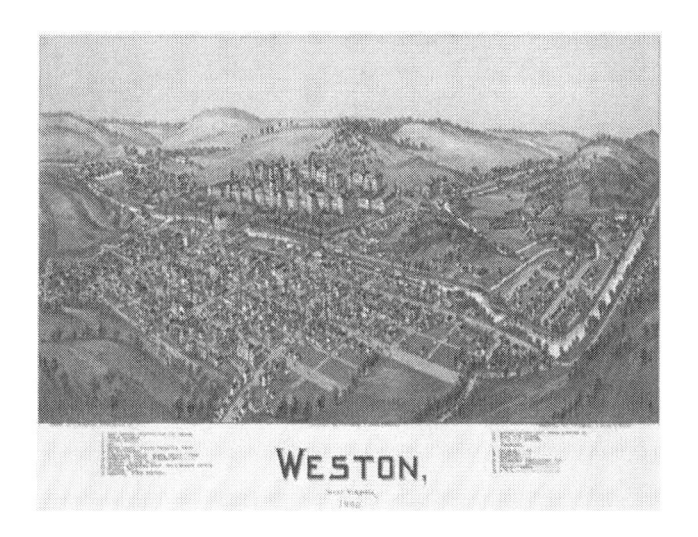

The troops arrived in Weston early on Sunday morning June 30, 1861. The Exchange Bank was located in the ground floor on the corner of Center and Bank Street. The banks cashier found himself facing three rifles and a suggestion that the vault be opened and gold coin be quickly handed over. The banks cashier, who happened to be a union supporter, handed over twenty-seven leather bags, each holding $1000 in gold coin. The bags were then transported across the river by wagon to the construction site of the new asylum. The Seventh Ohio Infantry set up camp on the grounds and spent the night before taking the money to Clarksburg on the very next day. The gold was then transported by train to Wheeling were it would be used to finance the 'Reorganized Government of Virginia.' It is believed that without these extra funds the government might not have been capable to establish the newly formed state of West Virginia.

The asylum's original troubles were only amplified by the situation between the two Virginias. West Virginia had to pay war reparations to Virginia, including the $27,000 snatched from the Exchange Bank, plus the original money Virginia had appropriated for the asylum. Virginia sent some of the patients who had been housed in its Staunton and Williamsburg facilities to Weston and charged West Virginia $23,000 for maintaining them from the time of its statehood (June 20th, 1863) to January 1st of 1866.

After Abraham Lincoln proclaimed the new state hood of West Virginia, the name of the asylum was altered to the "West Virginia Hospital for the Insane". This name would remain until 1913 when it would be changed to the Weston State Hospital. A total of four name changes would occur over the life of the hospital. Work would continue throughout the rest of the War Between the States with its completion in 1881.

View on Lawn at Hospital for Insane, Weston, W. Va.   Pub. by The Gizzy Studio, Weston, W. Va.

1899 vintage postcard

In 1863, a report to the state of West Virginia from the Board of Directors describes the progress of the building's construction. There was a nearly completed one-story section that had a length of 220 feet and was 29 feet wide. The hospital had three wings spanning from the center section at a right angle. Each of these wings was 120 feet long with two wings being 27 feet wide and the other 19 feet wide. A total of three cupolas would provide ventilation (and some decoration) for this section of the building. A kitchen, a boiler house, and a laundry area were constructed. A sewer was put in and it was said to be quite a job in itself. There was extensive work on the grounds done with excavation, site leveling, grading and the removal of rocks. The construction of the largest stone cut building in America was turning out to be a mammoth job as anticipated.

Regardless of its massive size, there are architectural details everywhere. There is beautiful detail in the stonework with human faces gracing the exterior of the civil war section of the building. Carvings of dogwood flowers on the exterior give a nod to the mother state of Virginia. In addition, one cannot ignore the central clock tower as it reaches some 200 feet into the air. With a Seth Thomas clock on four sides controlled by weights, the tower was a little too heavy and later was in need of repairs.

When the building was completed in 1881 it was 1295 feet long and occupied nine acres of floor space. The sandstone walls which were quarried locally were an astounding 2 1/2 feet thick. A total of 906 doors and 921 windows grace the building as well as a full basement, which runs the length of the building. How would you heat such a building? The heating system had a twelve-foot fan and engine that were installed in a building that was built about seventy-five feet from the main hospital building. The state-of-the-art system could change out the air in the entire hospital in less than four minutes. In the cold winters of the mountain state, the system brought heat and in the hot summers, it brought much appreciated cool air. It was a costly project and heating such a facility was extremely expensive. Coal was used to heat the building at first. However, in 1902 natural gas was found near the hospital and was immediately hooked up, creating a savings of roughly $5,000 per year for the state. In 1887, another new building was completed and was quickly filled by patients. The death of patients constituted the need of a cemetery, which was soon laid out. The total cost of the main hospital building was $625,000 with another hundred thousand dollars being spilt on the land and other buildings.

The Trans-Allegheny Lunatic Asylum was truly a gem of the Kirkbride plan. No hospital in the entire nation was more substantially built. The hospital had the first electric service in the community and it was generated on the very property they also had first telephone in the area. In the early years, the entire staff lived on the grounds. The building would evolve gradually just as the treatment plan would. When the hospital was first constructed the treatment plan was to provide a restful and quiet institution where the patients could enjoy solitude. Friends and family were discouraged from visiting their family members. Much later on in the late 19th century, work would be considered therapeutic. Patients would often work in the kitchen, on the ground with landscaping or in the wards with simple tasks. When the coalmine was operating, many patients became excellent coal miners. Everyone who was physically able to work had chores.

Many buildings were erected on the property as the years passed and other needs arose. In this report in 1916 during World War I, Henry Hurd helps one get a glimpse into exactly how self-sufficient the asylum was beginning to become.

Henry Hurd Report of 1916

The grounds belonging to the hospital contain about 335 acres, and front about 2000 feet on the West Fork River, opposite the town of Weston, and extend back to the north to a depth sufficient for this acreage. With the exception of the site on which the buildings are located, which extends back from the river about 800 feet, the land is very steep and entirely unsuitable for tillage. A very small portion of it is used for gardening, but most was used for grazing.

There are two producing gas wells upon the property, supplying abundant gas for all the needs of the institution, which were discovered in an effort to secure water by boring deep wells. The water supply is something of a problem with this institution, because the only source of supply is the West Fork River. The recent erection of a very large reservoir upon a high point of the hill in the rear of the building has solved the question of storage. So much filtering is needed, however, that it is difficult to get the water entirely free from sediment. There are some shallow drilled wells upon the premises, which are of considerable value in times of drought.

The first patients were admitted in October 1864, but construction continued into 1881. The 200-foot central clock tower was completed in 1871, and separate rooms for African Americans were completed in 1873. The hospital was intended to be self-sufficient, and a farm, dairy, waterworks, and cemetery were located on its grounds, which ultimately reached 666 acres in area.

The general hospital building consists of a central portion—the administration building with wings extending on either side north and south. The corridors connect all the wards with each other and with the central building. The main building, erected of native blue sandstone, is 1290 feet in length and 125 feet deep. The auxiliary buildings are of brick and are located in the rear of the main buildings.

In the rear of the main building are:

1. The Atkinson Building, erected in 1897, three stories in height, containing three wards, all used for male patients.

2. A three-story brick building, containing two wards, one for male colored patients, the other for female colored patients.

3. A laundry building, occupied by the laundry, with a plumbing shop and power plant in the basement.

4. An electric powerhouse, a one-story brick building, containing the electric light machinery, ice plant and three cold storage rooms.

5. A patients' kitchen, 45 by 75 feet, equipped with the necessary outfit for the cooking, which must be done on a large scale for such an institution.

6. A sick patients' kitchen.

7. A bake shop, a one-story brick building, containing oven, dough mixer, engine and other necessary utensils.

8. A store room, a two-story brick building, the lower floor containing the main store room, clothes-cutting room and sewing room; the upper floor is used as an attendants' dining room, with kitchen attached. This building is in bad condition.

9. A morgue; the morgue is a stone building for the reception of the bodies of patients dying in the house.

10. A hose house; a small frame building containing all the hose and firefighting apparatus.

11. Greenhouses

12. Barn; this is a frame structure; part of it is used for horses and the remainder for cows.

The Trans-Allegheny Lunatic Asylum; to many people it appeared statuesque and beautiful, almost like a medieval castle stripped from the pages of a fairytale book. It was far from a fairytale to those souls committed here in the early years. We will soon discover some of its darker history….after the doors opened and the first patients were led to their iron beds.

6
The Patients

Lunatic
lu·na·tic
Origin Middle English: from Latin luna 'moon'
From the belief that changes of the moon caused intermittent insanity

My mind was racing as I glanced down the official list of reasons for committal at the asylum back in the 19th century. It appeared that the 'good ole' days'" were not so good if you had any of the following:

Imaginary Female Trouble
Jealousy
Menopause
Grief
Dog Bite
Novel Reading
Syphilis
Bad Whisky

Immoral Life
Brain Fever
Egotism
Tobacco and Masturbation
Parents Were Cousins
Fell Off Horse in War
Seduction
Small Pox
Dropsy
Female Disease

Wow. Where to start? I think I got lost at *Seduction*. Was this another old timey condition perhaps meaning adultery? While the startling list of reasons for admission at Trans-Allegheny Lunatic Asylum may give only a glimpse of what caused the patient to be sent there, it reveals a lot about society's attitudes. A theme quickly emerges in the list showing how women in particular, were at the mercy of their husbands and families. He could sign her in as a patient and leave her until he decided to come back and get her released or until she died, whichever came first.

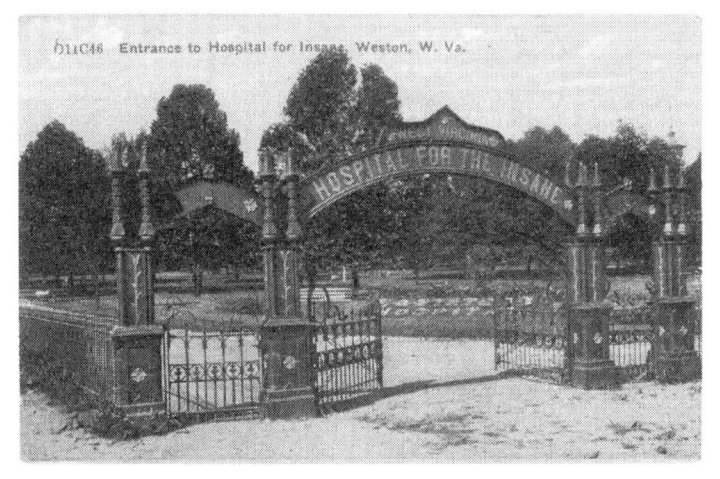

Vintage postcard, from the author's collection

The doors to the Trans-Allegheny Lunatic Asylum were opened in 1864 and the admissions began rolling in. On October 22, the first nine patients were admitted and all of them were female. One was just twenty-nine years old and single with her occupation being listed as a housekeeper from Monongalia County VA/WV. Her condition was listed as 'grief', which she had suffered from for two and half years with her form of insanity being listed as 'dementia'. She later died after living just two years at the hospital.

Patient number two was younger as well, being a single woman at the age of twenty-six. Her admitting diagnosis was "hereditary form of insanity" with the dementia beginning at age twenty-one. She was also a housekeeper from Harrison County, Virginia. Patient number three was also in her twenty's with her form of insanity being listed as 'dementia'. Her initial attack starting when she was just nineteen years of age. She was a resident from Upshur County. Patient number four was age twenty-seven, single and in ill health. She was suffering from melancholy and her occupation was listed as milliner. She hailed from Ohio County VA/WV.

TABULAR STATEMENT OF ALL UNDER TREATMENT DURING THE YEAR 1865.

#	Date of Admission	Sex	Age	Social Condition	Number Attacks	Duration of Insanity	Supposed Cause	Form of Insanity	Age at first attack	Homicidal	Hereditary	Occupation	Nativity	Residence	Result
1	Oct. 22	F	29	Single	2	1	2½ yrs	Grief	Dementia	23			Housekeeper	Virginia	Mon'galia co.	Died.
2	"	F	26	"	1	1	5 "	Hereditary	"	21		H	"	"	Harrison "	Remains.
3	"	F	24	"	1	1	5 "	Unknown	"	19			"	"	Upshur "	Dis. Imp'd
4	"	F	27	"	2	1	1 "	Ill health	Melancholia	22			Milliner	"	Ohio "	Remains,
5	"	F	39	"	1	1	2 "	Unknown	Acute Mania	37			Housekeeper	Ireland	" "	"
6	"	F	37	Married	1	1	2 "	Domestic trouble	Dementia	35	S	H	"	Virginia	" "	"
7	"	F	29	"	1	1	3 "	Ill health	Acute Mania	26			"	"	Kanawha "	"
8	"	F	22	Single	1	1	9 mos	Dysmennorrhia	"	21			"	Switzerl'd	Ohio "	"
9	"	F	33	Married	1	1	10 "	"The War,"	Acute Dem.	32			"	Virginia	Brooke "	"
10	Nov. 1	F	43	"	1	1	10 "	Ill health	Melancholia	43	S	H	"	"	Lewis "	Improved.
11	Nov. 16	F	34	"	1	1	2 yrs	Unknown	Acute Mania	32	S		"	"	Marion "	Remains.
12	Nov. 17	M	54	"	1	1	1½ "	Sun stroke	Melancholia	53	S		Cooper	Penn'a	Marshall "	"
13	Nov. 18	F	41	Single	3	1	2 "	Hereditary	Acute Mania	21		H	Spinster	Virginia	Harrison "	"
14	Nov. 25	F	28	Married	2	1	2 mos	Affliction	"	20	S	H	H Housekeeper	Penn'a	Ritchie "	Recovered.
15	Nov. 30	F	50	"	1	1	6 yrs	Unknown	Monomania	50		H		Germany	Ohio "	Remains.
16	Dec. 8	M	25	Single	1	1	8 "	Masturbation	Dementia	22			Farmer	Virginia	Gilmer "	"
17	Dec. 9	M	46	Married	1	1	2½ "	Trouble	Acute Mania	43		H	Carpenter	"	Ohio "	"
18	Dec. 16	F	36	"	1	1	9 "	Dissipated husb'd	Dementia	27			Housekeeper	"	Harrison "	"
19	Dec. 23	M	27	Single	1	1	4 "	Onanism	"	23		H	Laborer	"	Ritchie "	"
20	Dec. 27	M	38	Married	1	1	2 "	"The War,"	"	36			Merchant	"	Mason "	"
21	Dec. 30	M	38	Single	1	1	6 mos	Gen'l paralysis	"	38			Clerk	Penn'a	Ohio "	Died.
22	Jan. 3	M	22	Married	2	1	6 wks	"A fit,"	Acute Mania	16			Farmer	Virginia	Wirt "	Recovered.
23	Jan. 4	F	35	Single	1	1	32 yrs	Epilepsy	"	3			None	"	Tyler "	Died.
24	Jan. 10	M	20	"	1	1	6 mos	Fever & hered'try	Acute Dem.	20		H	Farmer	"	Marion "	Recovered.
25	Jan. 22	F	68	Married	1	1	16 yrs	Hereditary	Melancholia	52		H	Housekeeper	"	Ohio "	Improved.
26	Jan. 31	F	46	"	2	1	8 "	Uterine trouble	Acute Mania	42			"	Germany	Ohio "	Remains.
27	Feb. 12	M	23	Single	1	1	3 "	Masturbation	"	20			Cab't Mak'r	Virginia	Marion "	"
28	Feb. 28	M	35	Married	1	1	10 "	Hereditary	Chronic M'a	25	H		H Plasterer	"	Preston "	Eloped.

The admission book number one states that a Dr. Ralph Hill came to the hospital from Columbus, Ohio on October 19, 1864 and was in charge of the treatment of patients. It is interesting to note that the first eleven patients were female with ages ranging from twenty-two to thirty-nine.

In 1866, an overview of the institution stated that it was well on its way to becoming a city within itself. The large barn was very futuristic and even had running water, which was almost unheard of in that era. A boiler house was erected and the laundry building was nearly completed. All clothing and most of the furniture were made on the grounds using patient labor. Mattresses were made as well. The population in 1866 stood at eighty-two patients with forty males and forty-two females. Some of the diagnoses include dementia, acute mania, chronic mania, and melancholy. Some of the supposed causes were domestic trouble, the Great War, measles, religious excitement, and hereditary insanity.

Involuntary and voluntary admissions continued to appear through the doors. In an 1885 newspaper report, we have this case admission; 'Squire Sterling, dumped a violent, insane woman (Mrs. Lytle) at the asylum even though staff told him there was no room for her. The woman subsequently ended up in jail, where three or four men were forced to restrain her at times. She refused food, and someone administered food through a stomach pump. She died within a week. A month later, a twenty- five old woman at the asylum committed suicide by fastening a strip of bedding to the transom of her door." The newspaper reporting the suicide noted that "she has nine blood relatives at the Hospital."

In my research of this project I came across many interesting admission diagnoses. Monomania was found as the admitting diagnosis for a few interesting patients. In 19th psychiatry, monomania was described as a form of partial insanity in an otherwise perfectly sound mind. Types of obsession exist that are not considered normal. There are several variants to this condition; Erotomania exists when the patient is obsessed and believes that someone loves them. Kleptomania, of course, is the irresistible urge to steal and pyromania is the impulse to deliberately start fire. Lypemania was another form and it eventually became known as bi-polar disease. Anorexia nervosa is also a type if monomania where the patient has a fear of becoming overweight and feels the need to remain 'thin'. To give some examples of monomania in popular culture you would find that Edgar Allan Poe used this form of obsession with several of his stories. In *The Tell-Tale Heart* there is a madman who is obsessed with an elderly man's "vulture eye". *The Masque of the Red Death* is another example of obsession where the prince fears a terrible disease but finally contracts the disease and dies. Another example of obsession in the form of Erotomania would be that of Cecelia Rose in central Ohio. Cecelia killed her family by poisoning them with arsenic when they did not agree with her after she told them of her love of a next-door boy. Cecelia believed this love existed even when the boy himself told her it did not.

One such patient admitted for monomania is Thomas Phillips. Thomas became an admission to the asylum on November 25, 1891. He was listed as a widowed African-American blacksmith when he was admitted. Thomas must have had a serious condition as "no lucid intervals" were noted. It was also transcribed that he was violent to himself and others and he needed to be restrained to prevent injury. He died 'in a fit' April 19 of 1892, a short five months later.

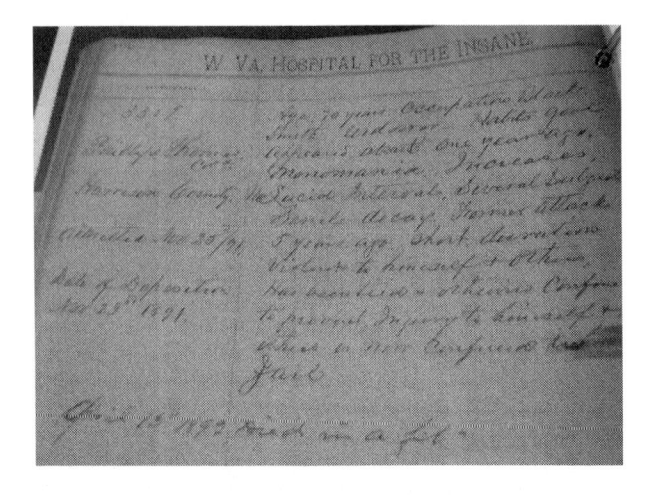

The admission record for Thomas Phillips
Photo by the author 2014

    I discovered a wonderful research source written by Kim Jacks. I stumbled across this while researching and wanted to include reference to this thesis as an invaluable source. In the lengthy thesis, Ms. Jacks states: "A visit to the hospital by the editor of the Wheeling Register resulted in an account reprinted in the Weston Democrat in 1871. He reported 242 patients residing there in eight wards, or hallways. All bedrooms were nine feet by twelve feet in size and opened to the hall. Each ward had a parlor, dining room, and bathroom. He described everything as very clean, neat, and pleasant. The rooms were light and cheerful and the "inmates" clean.
    He went on to describe some of the patients that he met: "Like all other institutions of this kind, the asylum at Weston had its celebrities. One man thinks himself the creator of the universe and delivers or rotations and toast that are wonderful for their pomposity and extravagant incoherence. He attempted to prove to Governor Jacob and the Board of Directors and the visitors who were present last Thursday that the elephant is the greatest and first of all Gods, and he summoned the turtle in as his witness. Another man has two ribs which he says are from the body of Adam. He carries them with him, tied by a leather thong. Another insists that he is dead and his importunate in his demand to be burned up. He says that he has to be burned up sometime and it might as well be done at once. A woman about forty years of age imagines herself a baby of about six months and cries and bawls to perfection. Some of the patients are suicidal and have to be carefully watched. Others are homicidal and have to be restrained. A large majority of them are peaceably disposed but are utterly incapable of taking care of themselves." This piece by the editor gives us a sampling of the

variety of psychosis present at the time of the visit. It was an interesting insight to a typical day at the asylum.

To some that were admitted, perhaps the asylum was seen as a welcome refuge from a cruel world and a broken heart. Lost loves, unfaithful spouses and widows seemed a common thread in a few admissions. And then you have those who suffered from religious excitement, such as Miss Hardy.

> **CRAZY ON RELIGION.**
>
> Miss Rose Hardy, of Parkersburg, Loses Her Reason Shortly Before the Date of Her Wedding.
>
> PARKERSBURG, W. Va., April 18.—Miss Rose Hardy, a beautiful young woman, daughter of a wealthy citizen living near here, was placed in the Weston asylum a raving maniac. For some weeks she attended ardently a series of religious meetings, and found at their close that her mind was gone. A week ago she was missed from her home, and four days later men who had been searching found her in the woods, evidently having suffered much from exposure and hunger. She was brought here, adjudged insane, and taken to Weston. It is reported that her wedding day had been set before the opening of the religious meetings.

Another interesting admission
Piqua Daily Leader April 18 1892

In 1871, the asylum was half completed and held around three hundred patients. Children were being admitted as well as adults. It was almost becoming an orphanage of sorts, That same year, the asylum accepted a seven-year-old girl who had become insane five months earlier due to (supposed) menstruation problems, a thirteen-year-old girl and two fifteen year old boys as well. Figures are incomplete, but the asylum accepted at least nine patients aged fifteen or under by 1880, including an eight year old boy who had been insane since he was three. (According to his mother) While researching the names in the cemeteries, I noticed several ages of children with many being under the age of twelve. It pulls at the strings of your heart when you think of the asylum children. Many were simply just innocent victims of a misunderstood condition at that time.

Patients could recover and leave or spend the rest of their lives at the asylum. Unfortunately, there were also those who took their own lives.

Whether out of desperation, schizophrenia, fear of spending their entire life in the hospital, or those who had 'broken hearts'. Isabella Brown was only twenty-five years old when she took her own life. She tied a sheet over the top of her door and thru the transom above. This was where she was found dead. She was not living alone at the asylum as a few of her family called it home as well. Some admissions state multiple family members as living at the hospital.

Hanging seems to be the most prevalent cause of death among the suicides listed. The very structure of some of the rooms at the hospital made hanging fairly easy. Water pipes can often be seen running along the ceilings of some of the rooms. These pipes are sturdy enough and high enough to hold a person's body weight and sheets were plentiful. Patients who were desperate enough could even hang themselves by their room doorknobs. Where this is a will, there is often a way. Perhaps the oddest death at the asylum occurred in 1896 when a patient fell into a box with about three inches of mortar in it. Cause of death was suffocation.

Admissions to the hospital since its opening gradually grew and grew until it was obvious it was suffering from overcrowding. Several applications for admissions of African-Americans had been denied early on in hospital history. They were refused because the administration did not have adequate rooming as these 'colored' patients needed to be kept separate from the whites. I was not until 1873 that a brand new building was built for segregation of African-Americans.

As the years passed and the population grew, conditions deteriorated rapidly. Accusations of mistreatment and mismanagement plagued the asylum and when an anonymous letter reached the office of the Wheeling Intelligencer in the early 1800s, Dr. Bland the superintendent, was under attack. Like the other large institution in the state, the West Virginia penitentiary, the public was learning more and more about these large buildings and mistreatments of prisoners and patients. Employees were similarly suffering from the conditions as you might presume.

Thousands of employees who worked at the hospital were taxed by long hours and difficult conditions. Most workers lived at the hospital and started their day at 6 am on the floor. Many doctors and nurses resided at the hospital as well. Like any facility, the majority of workers were kind and attending. They truly cared about the patients and tried to do the best they could with what supplies and sources they could utilize.

A few select cases had happy conclusions. In the 1940s, we have a case regarding a woman who was admitted as a widow with two small children. She had been working outside of the home until she was in a very bad car accident. Her sister helped her out but she soon became depressed and despondent . After admission and some treatment, she eventually was able to return home, secure another job and raise her children.

It seems as if the bad cases outweigh the positive cases especially if you spend much time reading the newspapers. Before he resigned in 1949, Dr. Knapp took a group of newspaper reporters into the hospital to show them the crisis he had at hand. Considerably overcrowding was a major issue. Patients were sleeping in hallways or on the floors. In some areas bathrooms were very far and few in between, sometimes only one bathroom for over fifty people. Introducing the reporters to what the asylum was truly like was a necessary evil for Dr. Bland to instigate. He wanted the conditions to become public so that people could realize this was the fault of the state, not the staff. More funds were needed and they were required as soon as possible.

Within the next year or two, new treatment procedures would be developed and used which one would think, would result in more discharges and a hospital census decline. Not always the case. In the 1950s, the census started to soar and the census teetered around 2,400 people.

Women in the 1950s had much to fear if their spouse was yearning for wife number two. Many women were diagnosed with menopausal conditions. Some who were admitted, never left even after menopause was over. It wasn't uncommon for women in menopause to actually receive shock treatments. Men suffered with questionable diagnoses as well.

One patient admitted in the 1950's was a male who had a job working at a logging company. He was hit in the head by a tree branch which fractured his skull. His wife said he became childlike and that she could no longer care for him at home. He was taken to Weston and admitted. He contracted pneumonia and died within just a few weeks. Other patients were elderly perhaps suffering from dementia or Alzheimer's (not yet named a disease) and families could no longer care for them so they too, became a patient.

In the 19th century, new admissions to TALA were quickly beginning to add up. This table shows the number of new admission for males and females in the early decades of operation.

Annual admissions to the Trans-Allegheny Lunatic Asylum. Source: Report of the Directors, Superintendent, and Treasurer of the West Virginia Hospital for the Insane for the years 1899-1900;

Year	Male	Female	Total
1864	6	15	21
1865	22	14	26
1866	6	8	14
1867	10	9	19
1868	93	69	162
1869	22	29	51

Year			
1870	11	31	42
1871	31	35	66
1872	55	31	86
1873	18	15	33
1874	56	34	90
1875	36	16	52
1876	72	52	124
1877	45	43	88
1878	36	21	57
1879	31	24	55
1880	67	61	128
1881	105	83	188
1882	93	106	199
1883	114	92	206
1884	97	79	176
1885	67	56	123
1886	63	41	104
1887	130	101	231
1888	112	104	216
1889	108	114	222
1890	128	105	233
1891	113	136	249
1892	137	88	225
1893	107	92	199
1894	110	85	195
1895	128	103	231
1896	106	87	193
1897	91	108	199
1898	133	113	266
1899	90	85	175
1900	38	31	69
Total	2707	2316	5023

INSANE ASYLUM HORRORS.

Suicide Followed Suicide in Southern State.

Men Boiled Themselves to Death or Hung by Ropes From Windows.

Fearful Charges of Neglect Against the Guards and Management.

PARKERSBURG, W. Va., Sept. 5.—A detailed account of the horrors at the Weston Insane Asylum in this State has been made public.

Suicide has followed suicide, it is charged, for some time among the inmates, and they have all been attended by the most horrible circumstances.

Men have killed themselves by boiling to death, and suspension by ropes from the windows.

All this has been done in sight of the guards, and no investigation has been made.

There seems to have been no inquests held on the dead, and a general inefficiency is manifested in the management.

Boston Globe September 5 1891

The census was growing yearly. Conditions were beginning to deteriorate and newspapers across the nation were picking up horrific stories such as this one. Bad news always travels fast and this shocking article above can attest to that with it reaching the front page of the Boston Globe in 1891. Aggressive and violent patients could be expected to be put into isolation or seclusion cells if warranted. The staff was expected to keep patients fed, dressed and bathed and above all, under control. The isolation cells were used when all else failed. They are located on the third floor and are an imposing reminder of what must have been pure hell for a patient and a necessary evil for the staff.

This door MUST have a story behind it.
Photo by author 2013

Seclusion cell in 2014
Photo by author

Music calms the savage beast, the old saying goes. Psychiatrists began to use the soothing effect of music on asylum patients in the 19th century. Concerts and dances were held in the auditorium located on the third floor in the main hospital. It has been proven that music can relieve stress and promote relaxation. Emotional states and pain sensitivity are also susceptible to modification through music therapy. Plays would take place on occasion with patients and staff acting out the roles. It is comforting to know that patients had healing therapies available such as this. The noises of an asylum were surely frightening at times. Screams, cries and the echo of slamming doors had to be extremely depressing.

The auditorium in 2014
Photo by the author

7
Drill the Skull and Ice the Body

Early treatments for various psychoses ranged from barbaric to unbelievable. Evidence abounds of inhumane treatment of the mentally ill throughout history. Though it is easy to judge early interventions harshly, looking back can help us keep an evolving field in perspective. Of course, descriptions of these treatments may cause you to shudder in horror that such a barbaric 'cure' was actually used on living human beings.

In the 18th century, some believed that mental illness was a moral issue that could be treated through humane care and instilling moral discipline. Strategies included hospitalization, isolation, and discussion about an individual's wrong beliefs.

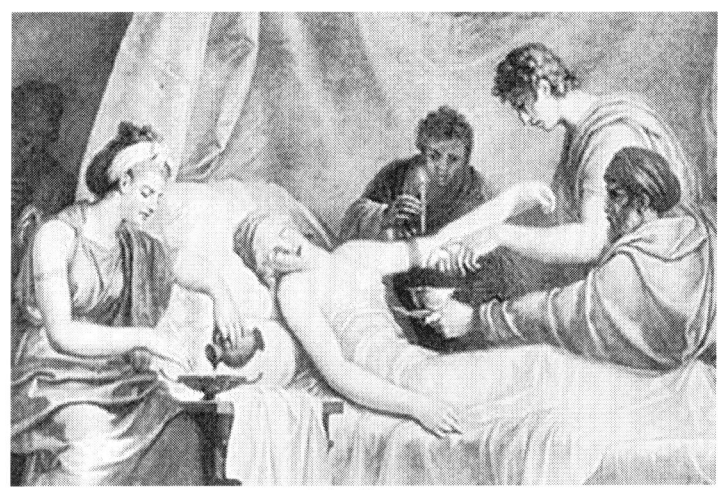

Bloodletting

Blood letting

Bloodletting originated in the ancient civilizations of Egypt and Greece, persisted through the Medieval, Renaissance, and Enlightenment periods, flourished in Arabic and Indian medicine, and lasted through the second Industrial Revolution. You can find it mentioned in the journals and diaries of America's founding fathers. Even George Washington had the practice applied to himself. The history of Bloodletting or Bleeding is vast and was intensely popular for about 2,500 years until it was replaced by the techniques of modern medicine. Doctors would bleed you for arthritis, back pain, headaches and general melancholia. The procedure was simple but crude. Most blood letters would open a vein in the arm, leg or neck with small, fine knife called a lancet. They would tie off the area with a tourniquet and, holding the lancet delicately between thumb and forefinger, strike diagonally or lengthwise into the vein. Blood would be measured and collected in bowls. Eventually the practice died, although it continued in some parts of rural America into the 1920s.

Fixing Humors

The Ancient Greek physician Claudius Galen believed that almost all ills originated in out-of-balance humors, or substances, in the body. In the 1600s, English physician Thomas Willis adapted this approach to mental disorders, arguing that an internal biochemical relationship was behind most mental disorders he had encountered in his practice. Bleeding, purging, and even vomiting were thought to help correct those imbalances and help heal physical and mental illness. Bleeding was used in the early days of treatment at TALA.

Woodcut of an exorcism 1598

Exorcism and Prayers

Due to a misunderstanding of the biological underpinnings of mental illness, signs of mood disorders, schizophrenia, and other mental woes have been viewed as signs of demonic possession in some cultures. As a result, mystic rituals such as exorcisms, prayer, and other religious ceremonies were used in an effort to relieve individuals and their family and community of the suffering caused by these disorders.

Trepanation

From the Neolithic era to the early 20th century, cultures all over the world used Trepanation as a way to cure patients of their ills. BY some estimates, this began over 7,000 years ago. Hippocrates endorsed its use and it is allegedly the world's second oldest surgical procedure following circumcision. Through the years, archaeologists have uncovered skulls marked by a carefully cut circular gap, which shows signs of being made long before the owner of the skull passed away. The holes were made by a saw, auger or by a hand drill boring thru the cranium. These fractures found in recovered skulls, were no accident; they were the result one of the earliest forms of psychiatric treatments. In early days, it was believed that the devil or demons, could take up residence in one's head. The way to relieve ones head of the evilness or impurities? Simple. Drill a hole through the skull and let the evil out. An instrument called a trepan is used to make the hole. The trepan goes into your skull and a chunk of your skull is extracted. Eventually the skin heals over the hole and you are left with a small bump. Although no diagnostic manual exists from that time, experts guess that this procedure to remove a small section of skull might have been aimed at relieving headaches, mental illness, or presumed demonic possession.

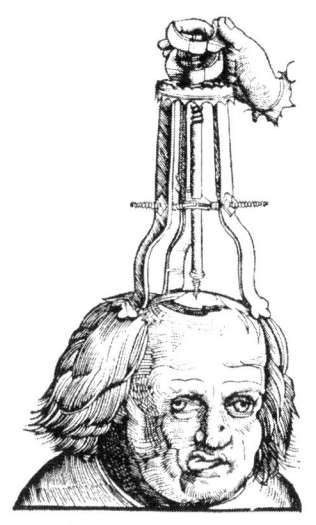

Trepanation sketch

Fever Therapy

The Ancient Greeks had observed that a period of fever sometimes cured people of other symptoms, but it was not until the late 1800s that fevers were induced to try to treat mental illness. Austrian psychiatrist Julius Wagner-Jauregg infected a syphilis patient with malaria and the resulting fever cured the patient of the psychosis caused by his syphilis.

Hysteria Therapy

Back in the ancient times, women suffering from any type of mental illness were lumped together as victims of hysteria. The Greek physician Hippocrates popularized the term 'hysteria' but Plato questioned his thinking. Hippocrates believed hysteria encompassed conditions ranging from nervousness to fainting fits to spontaneous muteness. The root cause, according to him, was a wandering womb. He claimed that if the woman's uterus "remains unfruitful long beyond its proper time, it gets discontented and angry and wanders in every direction through the body, closes up the passages of breath, and, by obstructing respiration, drives women to extremity." Plato's thoughts on the subject? He believed that the only sure way to solve the problem of hysteria was to get married and have children. The diagnosis of hysteria was still being used until the 20th century.

Hydrotherapy

Building off the idea that a bath is often calming, psychiatrists of years past attempted to remedy various symptoms with corresponding liquid treatments. For instance, hyperactive patients got hot, tiring baths, while lethargic patients received stimulating sprays with cold water. Some doctors, however, got a bit too excited about the idea, prescribing therapies that sounded more like punishment than therapy. One treatment involved wrapping the lucky patient up as if he were a mummy of sorts and then placing them in a bathtub filled with icy water. Unbelievably, this is where we get the phrase "chill out". Another treatment required the patient to remain continuously submerged in a bath for hour's even days-which might not sound so bad, except they were strapped in and only allowed out to use the bathroom.

Some doctors ordered the use of high-pressure jets. Sources indicate that at least one patient was strapped to the wall in the crucifixion position (never a good sign) and blasted with water from a fire hose. Like many extreme treatments, hydrotherapy was eventually replaced with psychiatric drugs, which tended to be more effective and much more pleasant for many.

Mesmerizing Treatment
Austrian physician Franz Mesmer suggested that an invisible force pervaded everything in existence, and that disruptions in this force caused great pain and suffering. Mesmer thought the use of magnets could aid in this therapy. He believed that by placing magnets on certain areas of a patient's body might be able to counteract the disruptive influence of the moon's gravity and restore the normal flow of bodily fluids. Surprisingly, many patients praised the treatment as a miracle cure, but the medical community dismissed it as hogwash. Nonetheless, he ended up leaving his mark on the English language with the word *mesmerize*.

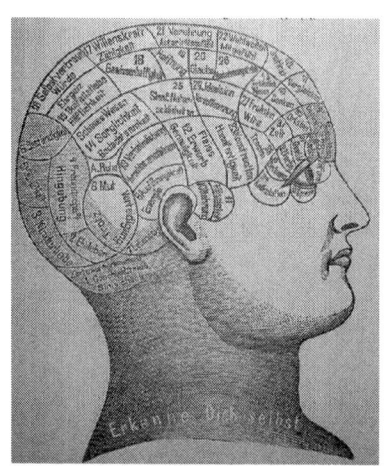

Phrenology sketch

Phrenology

German physician Franz Gall [wiki] developed phrenology, a practice based on the idea that people's personalities are depicted in the bumps and depressions of their skulls. I remember studying this in one of psychology classes many years ago. The idea that bumps, lumps and indentations in the skull could be a sort of road map to your personality intrigued me. Of course, this theory never really made it as a popular field of study, but it is fascinating. Basically, Gall believed that the parts of the brain a person used more often would get bigger, like muscles. Consequently, these pumped-up bigger areas would take up more skull space, leaving visible bumps in those places on your head. He then tried to determine which parts of the skull corresponded to which traits. For instance, bumps over the ears meant you were destructive; a ridge at the top of the head indicated benevolence; and thick folds on the back of the neck were signs of a sexually oriented personality. His theory was out by the early 1900's.

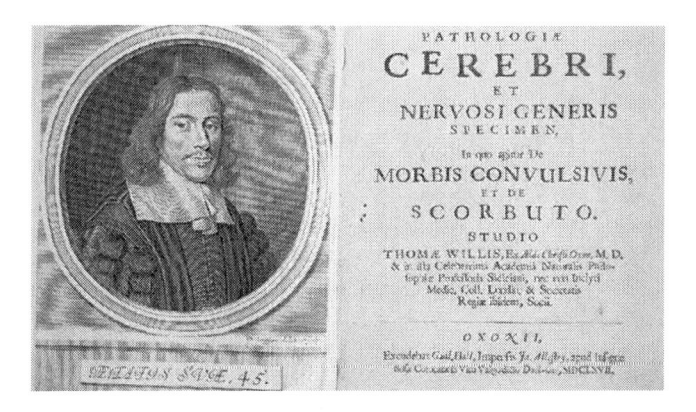

Rotational Therapy

Charles Darwin's grandfather Erasmus Darwin was a physician, philosopher, and scientist. Consequently, his ideas weren't always taken seriously as many questioned his status as a scientist since it was due to his theories being a bit far-fetched, such as his spinning-couch treatment aka Rotational Therapy.

Darwin's logic was that *sleep* could cure disease and that spinning around rapidly was a great way to induce slumber. Nobody paid much attention to it at first, but later, American physician Benjamin Rush adapted the treatment for psychiatric purposes. He believed that spinning would reduce brain congestion and in turn, cure mental illness. He was wrong. Instead, Rush just ended up with dizzy patients who were still crazy. These days, rotating chairs are limited to the study of vertigo and space sickness.

The spinning or rotating chair

Confinement

Confinement by the use of cribs, (also known as Utica cribs) chairs or isolation cells were used in many instances. Violent behaviors had to be contained to protect the staff as well as the patient. Some cribs were made out of intricately carved wood, many were made out of iron, and some were very crudely constructed. Patients would sleep in it for extended periods of time until a regulatory crackdown curtailed restraint use for all but the most uncooperative and violent patients.

Confinement crib from the Columbus Ohio Lunatic Asylum

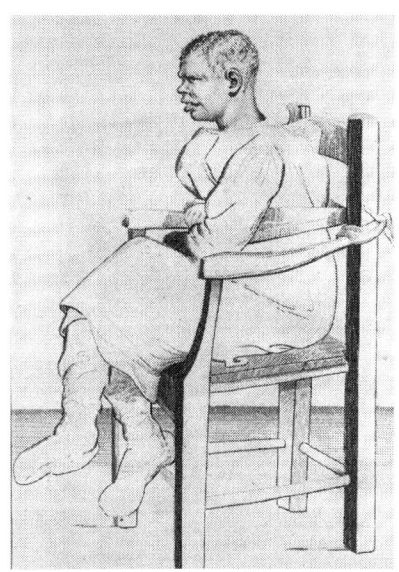

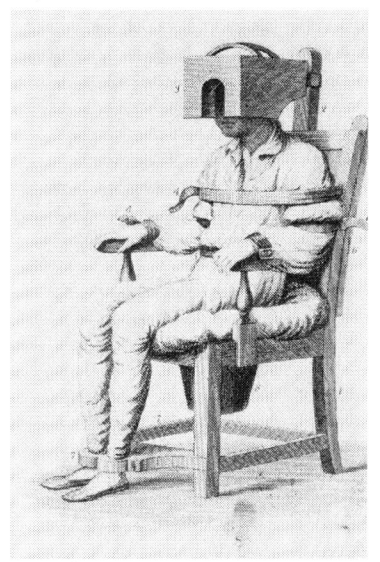

Confinement in chairs

Insulin Shock Therapy

The coma-therapy trend began in 1927. Viennese physician Manfred Sakel accidentally gave one of his diabetic patients an insulin overdose, and it sent her into a coma. However, what could have been a major medical faux pas turned into a triumph. The woman, a drug addict, woke up and declared her morphine craving gone. Then Sakel (who really is not earning our trust here) made the same mistake with another patient, who also woke up claiming to be cured. Regardless, the popularity of insulin therapy [wiki] faded, mainly because it was dangerous. Slipping into a coma is no walk in the park, and between one and two percent of treated patients died as a result. *(see Insulin Coma Therapy pg. 69)*

Lobotomy

Lobotomy is one of the most popular treatments asked about at the asylum. I recognize that inmates at the West Virginia Penitentiary, patients at Spencer State Hospital, TALA, Huntington State and other institutions in West Virginia, were subjected to this controversial and permanent procedure. (Former employees of Spencer State Hospital claim a staff doctor and "a thrown-together staff of hospital workers." crudely did the surgery.)

One of the few psychiatric treatments to receive a Nobel Prize, the lobotomy is also one that is now used infrequently. (Thankfully, I might add.) In 1949, Dr. Moniz received the Nobel Prize in Medicine for his work. Some lobotomy victims have called for Moniz's Nobel Prize to be recalled in past years. Lobotomy was the first psychiatry treatment designed to alleviate suffering by disrupting brain circuits that might cause symptoms. It was said to help disturbed patients with schizophrenia, manic depression and mania (bipolar disorder), and other mental illnesses.

A new way to do lobotomies gained popularity due to Dr. Walter Freeman. After experimenting with novel ways of performing these brain surgeries, Freeman formulated a new procedure called the transorbital lobotomy. It was quick and inexpensive to do. Freeman charged $25 for each procedure done. This new procedure became known as the icepick lobotomy and was performed by inserting a metal pick (like an ice pick) into the corner of each eye socket and moving it back and forth, severing the connections to the prefrontal cortex in the frontal lobes of the brain. This area controls emotion and aggression.

In the 1951 Board of Control Report at the asylum, it was reported that seventy transorbital lobotomies being performed and that Dr. Freeman was on site conducting post-operative exams. Forty were done from 1948-49 and five in 1949-1950 and none as of June 1959.

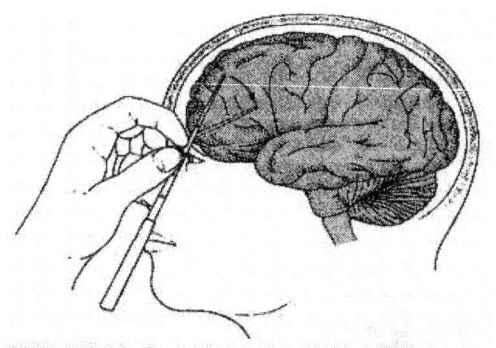

FIGURE 18.12 "Ice pick" prefrontal lobotomy. The sharp metal rod is inserted under the eyelid and just above the eye, so that it pierces the skull and enters the base of the frontal lobe. (Adapted from Freeman, W. Proceedings of the Royal Society of Medicine, 1949, 42 (suppl.). 8-12.)

Dr. Walter Freeman will forever have his name tied to this procedure chiefly due to his lobotomy tour of '52. He performed two hundred and twenty-eight transorbital lobotomies during a two-week period in 1952 in West Virginia, through a state-sponsored lobotomy project dubbed "Operation Ice Pick" by newspapers. Numerous newspapers across the state and country reported on the procedure and on the good doctor's approach. One account says, "Freeman devoted an intensity and energy to his mission in West Virginia that surpassed nowhere else. Over the next four years he frequently visited the state, with the result that its per capita rate of lobotomy was the highest in the nation." The New York Times even reported on the subject and remarked that Dr. Freeman was on a crusade to teach his technique to doctors in America. Time magazine announced, "By the time he finished his experiments with patients in West Virginia mental hospitals last month, Washington Neurologist Walter Freeman had supervised or performed more than 200 of these transorbital lobotomies in two weeks." That story ran on May 29 1951 issue of TIME.

'Operation Icepick' Begun
State Starts Brain Surgery on Mass-Production Level As Noted Doctor Operates on 16 Mental Patients

Charleston Gazette July 20 1952

To give him some due credit, Philadelphia born Freeman was a member of the American Psychiatric Association and he is credited with perfecting the lobotomy procedure in the 1940's. His memoir states that he personally performed 3,439 lobotomies in twenty-three states with his youngest patient being just four years old. Some sources tout him as being a bit of an oddball and theatrical at times when operating. His most famous lobotomy was performed on President John F. Kennedy's sister Rosemary Kennedy. It left her with severe mental and physical disability. Freeman died in 1972.

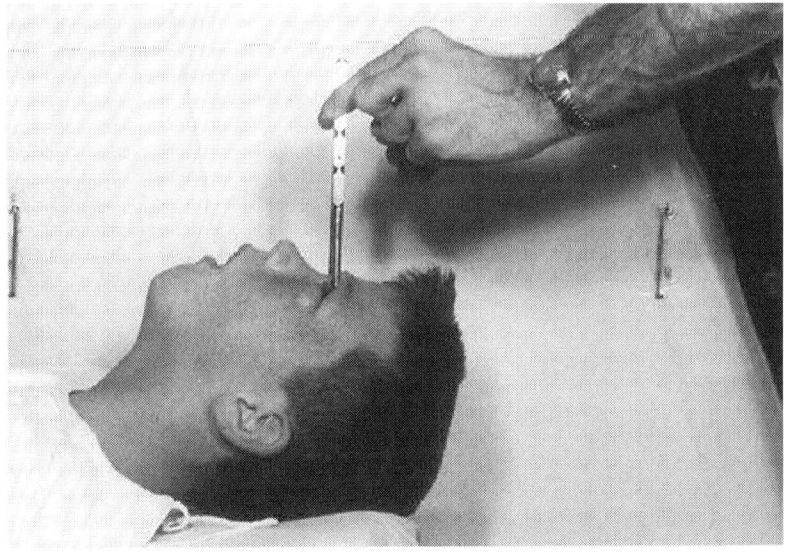

Transorbital Lobotomy

The practice gradually fell out of favor beginning in the mid-1950s, when antipsychotics, antidepressants, and other medications that were much more effective in treating and alleviating the distress of mentally disturbed patients came into use. Today lobotomy is rarely performed.

Side effects of lobotomy:
Possible death
Loss of motor function
Incontinence
Epilepsy
Loss of cognitive function
Loss of emotion and personality
Lack of tact and discipline
Lack of empathy

Icepick Surgery Continues

HUNTINGTON (P)—Dr. Walter J. Freeman will return to Huntington State Hospital Friday to perform about 60 more transorbital lobotomies, commonly called "icepick." operations.

The George Washington University professor is consulting neurosurgeon to West Virginia mental hospitals. He said he expects to perform about 300 of the operations in the state this month.

"Icepick surgery" is supposed to ease mental tension. A long slender instrument is inserted beneath the upper eyelid to sever certain nerves in the front part of the brain.

Dr. Freeman has conducted 87 operations at Weston State this year, 19 at Spencer, 31 at Lakin and 22 at Huntington State. Of 232 patients operated on last summer, he said, about 100 have improved enough to be sent home.

The Charleston Daily Mail July 15 1953

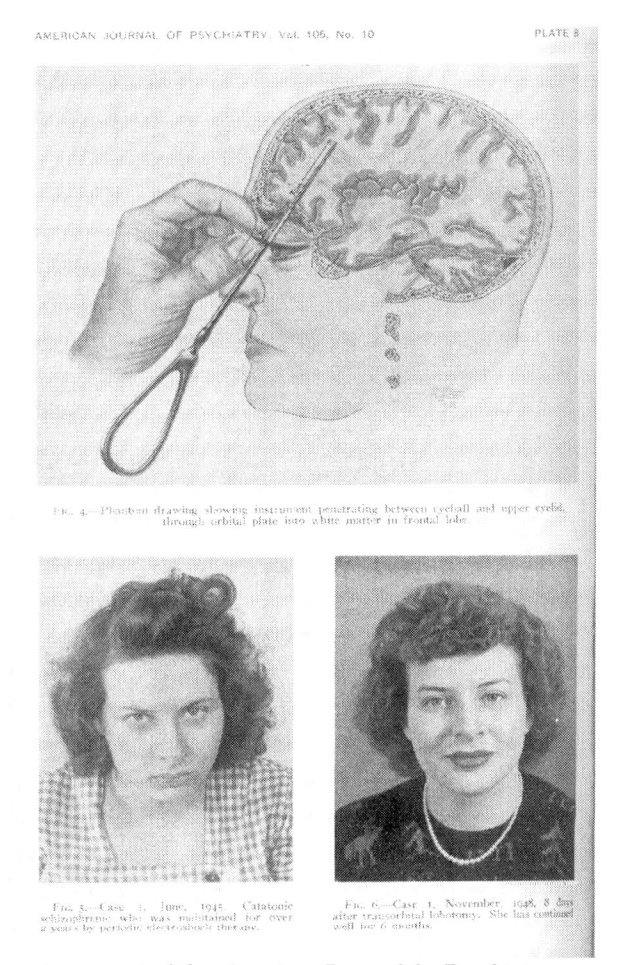

A page out of the American Journal for Psychiatry showing the effects of lobotomy

Restraints & Isolation

Moral treatment was the overarching therapeutic foundation for the 18th century. However, even at that time, physicians had not fully separated mental and physical illness from each other. Asylums were places where people with mental disorders could be placed, allegedly for treatment, but often to remove them from the view of their families, friends and communities. As a result, some of the treatments in those days were purely physical approaches to ending mental disorders and their symptoms.

1848 sketch of asylum restraints

Malaria Therapy
Many admissions into asylums documented syphilis as a valid reason for committal. There was no cure for the sexually transmitted diseases in those early asylum days. In the early 1900s, a Viennese neurologist by the name of Wagner von Jauregg got the idea to treat syphilis sufferers with malaria-infected blood. Predictably, these STD patients would develop the disease, which would cause an extremely high fever that would kill the syphilis bacteria. Once that happened, they were given the malaria drug Quinine; they were cured and sent home. The treatment did have its share of side effects -that nasty sustained fever, for one - but it worked and it was a whole lot better than dying. In fact, Von Jauregg won the Nobel Prize for malaria therapy, and the treatment remained in use until the development of penicillin came along and gave doctors a better, safer way to sure the STD.

Insulin Coma Therapy

Deliberately creating a low blood sugar coma gained attention in the 1930s as a tool for treating mental illness. It was popular because it was believed that dramatically changing insulin levels could alter the wiring in the brain. This treatment lasted for several more decades, with many practitioners swearing by the positive results for patients who went through this treatment. The comas lasted for one to four hours, and the treatment faded from use during the 1960s.

Metrazol Therapy

This was an early type of electro convulsive therapy. As the understanding of mental illness evolved, some practitioners came to believe that seizures from such conditions as epilepsy and mental illness (including schizophrenia) could not exist together. So seizures were deliberately induced using medications like the stimulant Metrazol (withdrawn from use by the FDA in 1982) to try to reduce mental illness. These seizures were not effective, nor were the outcomes of the treatments. Researchers later realized that epilepsy and schizophrenia are not mutually exclusive. This field of seizure-related therapies later led to the more effective study of electric shocks and ECT.

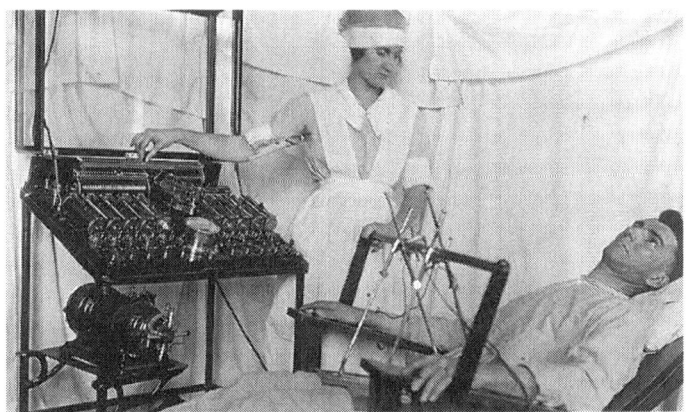

Electroconvulsive therapy (ECT)

Electroconvulsive therapy is a procedure in which electric currents are passed through the brain, intentionally triggering a brief seizure. It was first developed in 1938. ECT seems to cause changes in brain chemistry that can quickly reverse symptoms of certain mental illnesses. It often works when other treatments are unsuccessful.

In the early days of this therapy, high doses of electricity were administered without anesthesia resulting in broken bones, memory loss, and other serious side effects. Patients in the 1950s would often receive around 100 treatments and at a much higher voltage than used today. In 1951 Board of Control report, at the asylum, a new electro shock machine was ordered. They had been using two machines daily on both the female and the male side of the hospital and that these patients would receive three treatments per week. Common side effects after today's standard treatment of ECT is applied are headache, stomachache and muscle aches.

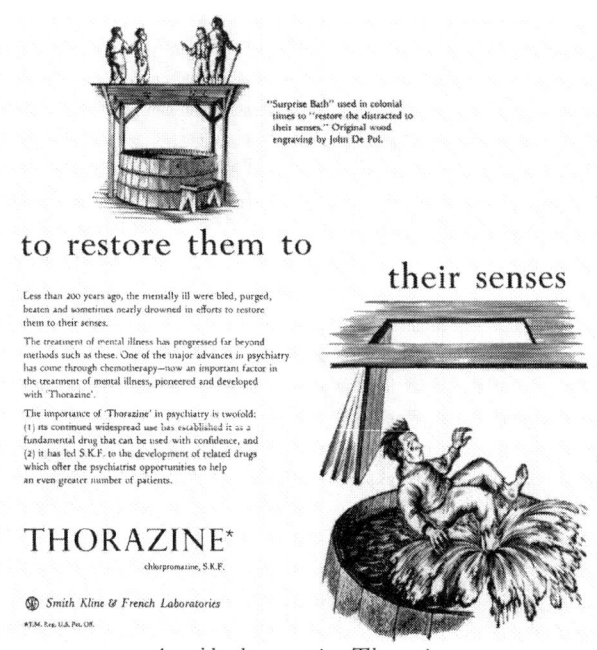

An old ad promoting Thorazine

Thorazine
In the 1950's, the introduction of anti-psychotic drugs such as chlorpromazine (thorazine) offered patients an alternative form of treatment, and began to eliminate the need for the drastic treatments such as the lobotomy and ECT. Thorazine was first created by a team of French researchers who were aiming for a cure for malaria. Although they were unsuccessful in their attempts, they did discover that the drug had sedative side effects. Thorozine was reported to reduce aggressive behavior, anxiety, hallucinations and the desire to self-mutilate or harm others, and quickly other drugs based around its chemical compound were being produced in large amounts. Thorazine ultimately became known as the 'Medicinal Lobotomy'.

8
The Staff

Dr. Ralph Hills had been on staff at Central Ohio Insane Asylum (The Columbus State Hospital) since 1856. He became the asylum's first Superintendent. As work continued on the asylum, he accepted only a few patients during the first years of its operation. Some of the odder reasons for patient's committal included: jealousy, imprisonment, change of life, hard study, disappointment, perplexity, desertion by wife, loss of friends, accusation of arson, indigestion, loss of leg, worms, and superstition. However, many patients had no known livelihood, farmers and housekeepers were the two most prevalent occupations. Women were no more likely than men to be committed to the asylum.

Hills bragged continually about his low per capita costs: $132.56 in 1868 and $127.40 in 1870; by 1878, his successor had brought the figure down to $115.95. For comparison's sake, it was $249.60 at Central Asylum in Ohio and $179.92 at the Stockton Asylum in California. Throughout the nineteenth century, the asylum maintained its low patient expenditures while continually claiming to provide the best care possible.

Hills may have been an efficient manager, but the locals evidently found him unsatisfactory. The Weston Democrat noted at the time of Dr. Hills's departure in 1871, that the asylum would cease to be a "political football" and a "place for the manufacture of political capital." What prompted these remarks is unclear, but the story also stated that it was not suitable to "kick a man when he's down." The paper noted with satisfaction that in the new superintendent, Dr. Thomas Camden, the state of West Virginia had finally realized that a person within its own borders could successfully operate and manage the asylum.

Despite his long running favor with the paper, Camden could not escape his share of management problems. Overcrowding, which hurt both staff and patients, had become an issue for Hills and continued during Camden's tenure. He and successive superintendents at the asylum were aware of overcrowding's detrimental effects but felt tremendous pressure to take mentally ill people out of jails where they were otherwise held.

Things began to downward spiral quickly. Overcrowding was so bad that in 1878, Camden felt compelled to beg for a ventilating fan to remove the 'heavily carbonized' air that patients and staff were breathing and re-breathing. In the same report, he also begged for fire hoses and other equipment in case the asylum caught fire. In his 1880 report, Camden had cause for optimism. He noted that they had about emptied West Virginia's jails of their insane, bringing the number of patients at the asylum to 491.

When Dr. W. J. Bland took over in 1882, he had five hundred and eighty-nine patients, of which thirty-two were 'colored'. He urged that patients who needed help come to the asylum and stay there for as long as it took to recover. Sadly, he admitted, most of his patients were chronically insane because they had not received help when they needed it most—in the acute phase. Instead, they had languished in jails or at home, where their families could not provide the rigorous discipline and sound judgment necessary to affect a cure for them. Bland solidly opposed home care, believing that the home environment usually contributed to the patient's insanity in the first place.

By 1885, Bland administered to six hundred and eighty patients. Two women committed suicide that year, one by tying a pillowcase and handkerchief to her bedpost and leaning forward so that her body slipped under the bed. In 1886, another woman committed suicide by tying a sheet over the transom, and a male patient cut his throat when he was in a restraining bed. As with other suicides and accidental deaths at the asylum, officers and employees were exonerated from blame. At this point, Bland may have wondered if his $2,000 annual salary was worth it. Dr. Hills had received the same sum in 1864 but had far less responsibility. Assistant physician Dr. Stalnaker resigned in 1882, partially because of the "inadequacy of salary."

Dr. J. S. Lewis, who replaced Stalnaker at presumably at the same salary, later replaced Bland as superintendent. Though the move doubled his salary, Lewis may also have wondered if the aggravation was worth it. His exasperation comes through in 1891 when he lamented the sensational publicity given to an escaping patient's death. "The truth is so distorted that it would appear that you gentlemen, as well as we . . . are demons in human form and permit these things to occur for mere fun." Another patient died after being scalded in his bath, while another man committed suicide by hanging. Though the coroner was satisfied in all these cases, the public undoubtedly gossiped about them or hinted at darker truths.

By the end of fiscal year 1893, West Virginia Hospital for the Insane held nine hundred and forty-three patients under the supervision of another superintendent, Dr. W. P. Crumbacker. The asylum could provide little more than custodial care at that point, but Superintendent Crumbacker immediately abolished the cribs, sleeves, straps, and other physical restraints the asylum had been using. He complained that commitment officials were so sloppy they sometimes did not spell a patient's name twice the same way on their committal paperwork. Additionally, they seldom entered anything concerning what was wrong with patients, leaving asylum staff wondering how to best treat them. Crumbacker had a suicide on his hands almost immediately, as well as the death of a staff physician from typhoid. In July 1897, the asylum's entire administration, except for two board members, changed. Apparently, a much-needed change.

Dr. W. E. Stathers replaced Crumbacker. The asylum report for this period has nothing to say about why the changes occurred. At the end of fiscal year 1900, the hospital had nine hundred and ninety-eight patients, of whom seventy three were African-American. Stathers reported a cure rate of 48.8 percent and a mortality rate of 3.3 percent, both exceptional figures.

Stathers supported his patients on less than Hills did when the asylum opened in 1864. Stathers expended $129.36 per capita in 1898, against Hills's $132.56 in 1868. The asylum could not seem to control the number of patients coming in, so existing funds had to cover whatever increased expenses arose because of them, plus the shortfalls in legislative funding. Though the asylum seems to have avoided national scandals or any easily discovered reports of ill treatment, it could not have provided ideal care. As the asylum became further overcrowded and without an adequate increase in funding for patient welfare, conditions declined. Patients were probably ill fed and clothed by this time and likely received very little assistance from their caretakers.

I imagine temptation to steal is great to some when you are placed into the position of accounting and bookkeeping at a large institution with large sums of money flowing through your hands. Such was the case with Frank

MacAndrews in 1929. He was assigned the position at the asylum as bookkeeper. Eventually the temptation to steal won and he was convicted of embezzlement. He was sentenced to three years in the West Virginia Penitentiary in Moundsville. After serving only eight months, he was paroled for good behavior and he was transferred back to the asylum. Must have been great with numbers! I guess this is one case where leaving a prison and going to an asylum is a step up.

The staff of the asylum lived on the grounds in the early years. Twelve hour shifts were common and usually one day off was all that was enjoyed…per month. Average pay at the end of the 19th century was around twenty-five dollars per month. Of course living on site helped greatly with the cost of living. Staff continued living on site until the mid 1960's. A typical day began before 6am with staff rising from their beds. Nurse's apartments were located on the third floor of the main hospital building. Doctor's apartments were on the second floor. Some of the nurse's rooms resembled the dorm rooms at a college, complete with the sharing of bathrooms. Meals would be eaten at the asylum in a special dining room until the practice was eventually stopped. An increase in pay was given after meals were discontinued.

One staff member certainly worth noting would be Harriet B. Jones. Jones was the first woman physician to be licensed in the state of West Virginia. On May 1, 1884, she graduated with honors from the Women's Medical College at Baltimore, Maryland, as a physician and surgeon. In her long career, she was often publicized as "West Virginia's Foremost Woman". Two years as a general practitioner were followed by three years at the asylum as assistant superintendent. She was a leader of the Women's Right to Vote and was instrumental is the movement for the building of the West Virginia Tuberculosis Sanitarium in Denmar. She returned to

Wheeling after her time at the asylum and opened a hospital for women. Dr. Jones was also one of the first women to serve in the West Virginia Legislature. Her life long career in medicine, women's rights and service ended in 1943 when she passed from this earthly realm.

Charleston WV newspaper dated January 23 1949

Anyone who enters the medical field deserves a jewel in their crown as my grandmother used to say. It takes a special person to care for another and to do it well. Among all of the articles I found of mistreatment and scandal, there were those who truly cared about their work and about the patients welfare. The attendants, doctors, nurses, and other staff did the best they could with what resources they had at the time.

Weston Employes To Get Raises

CHARLESTON, W. Va. (AP) — Officials have been able to give employes at Weston State Hospital a 7.5 per cent pay raise with money from about 80 unfilled positions there.

Bluefield Daily Telegraph July 28 1974

It seemed as if the staff and doctors were occasionally put on the defensive with letters to various local newspapers concerning the care and upkeep of patients at the asylum. One such article is the one that graced the Charleston Gazette on September 26th 1975. It read, "The number of physicians on the hospital staff was sixteen as of September 1st and not three as stated in the letter to the editor. All physicians practicing at Weston State hospital are licensed. The number of psychologists on the staff of the hospital is nine, not eleven as given in the letter to the editor. The hospital staff includes the largest number of social workers and nurses that have ever been employed at institution. There are 750 employees at Weston State hospital, a group of dedicated faithful and hard-working people. They show a genuine concern for the welfare of the patients. Evidence of this concern is frequently noted in mentioned by visitors, friends, and relatives of patients. We do appreciate the writers appeal to citizens to help us improve the quality of care for patients. We agree that much improvement is to be made and we are doing all that we can with our available resources. All of our patients and employees appreciate legislative and citizen support of our total mental health system in the state of West Virginia and our Weston State Hospital in particular." Signed, W. O. Poling, Superintendent, Weston State Hospital.

Near the end of its use as an operating asylum, great strides and changes in attitudes had been made in psychiatry. The hospital emphasis switched to accurate assessment, proper treatment and restoration of optimal functioning. This became the norm. The old way of asylum life had been to provide custodial care. The hospital tried to evolve but the changes were difficult and time consuming although the hospital had made some strides in the right direction. Politics played a role as it often does in facilities such as this resulting in one-step forward and two-steps back.

The hospital had been organized into seven different specialized units of care. Changes had been made in admission and a person could be admitted, assessed and treated while only staying less than a month. Therapeutic services were added such as Patient Employment, Hygiene, Adaptive Skills, Therapeutic Recreation and Medical Diagnostic services to name just a few. In the early days of operation, family and friends were discouraged from visiting the committed. As the years passed, it was discovered to be therapeutic for people to visit and therapies improved as well-no more forcing patients to lie for hours wrapped tightly in sheets soaking in ice water. By the 1940's, new hydrotherapy was instituted. Tubs, showers and massage tables were utilized in a much more gentle and beneficial way. Like any field, psychiatry was evolving and changing…for the better.

During the course of research for this project, I had the chance to interview a few nurses who worked or did their clinicals at TALA. My mother-in-law, Linda Queener Adams remembers her experience at the asylum, as short lived as it was. "It was horrible. I was there for about two weeks and worked in about every department while doing my clinical's for nursing. What an experience! It almost made me rethink my career in nursing. I remember one young man who had just turned eighteen years old. They took him out of the adolescent unit and put him in the adult unit. He would lay in the hallway in his own body fluids all sprawled out and naked. I was there in the early 1970s when they had geographic units and everyone was separated, not by their diagnosis, but by what area they came from. You could have someone there with mild depression next to a more violent patient."

I interviewed several nurses and staff members for this book project. All were grateful for their job experience at the asylum…and most were happy to have moved on to other jobs and careers.

9
Reasons For Committal

In the late 19th and early 20th centuries, terms such as "madness," "lunacy" or "insanity"—all of which assumed a unitary psychosis—were split into numerous "mental diseases," of which catatonia, melancholia and dementia praecox (modern day schizophrenia) were the most common in psychiatric institutions

The treatment of patients in early lunatic asylums was sometimes brutal and focused on containment and restraints. How could a person end up in such an institution against their will? Reasons for committal were varied back in the early days at TALA. Older folks who had no one to take care of them, could simply walk into the hospital, sign some papers and stay till there this their dying day. Family members would often be embarrassed about their "slow" family member and have them become a resident as well. Boys and young men who were caught masturbating could be committed. Children who had ailments such as smallpox, heart disease such as mitral valve prolapse, exhaustion or tuberculosis could be committed. In 1912, twelve-year-old John Green was admitted and then died from epilepsy. He is buried in one of the asylum cemeteries. Teenager William

Lee Gumm died of tuberculosis in 1933. He is also buried in an unmarked grave.

Women who were pregnant and were soon to bare illegitimate children could be committed by her family simply out of shame. Such was the case of a young woman committed at TALA who was pregnant from rape…as a result from her stepfather. Amenorrhea was listed as a cause for committal as we see in the case of an eighteen-year-old young woman who was committed for 'Amenorrhea and Acute Mania'. Amenorrhea is the suppression or unusual absence of menstruation. She could have been pregnant, or suffered from a medical condition that was unknown at that time such as a glandular issue. Suspicions of crime or suicide are also alluded to in the list of Reasons for Committal. Among the admissions are entries for gunshot wounds, shooting a child and 'rumor of husband murder', whatever that entails.

A child's buggy silhouetted by an asylum window
Photo by author 2014

Other reasons to be admitted were; depression, alcoholism, just being a little different from the norm, and even going through menopause! It is apparent that menopause or 'change of life' was a popular reason for committal and the husband could simply sign a paper and leave his wife…and their children at the asylum forever or until he came back to sign them out. Note the case of admission number six in 1864. She was 87 years old and married. She was committed 'Domestic Trouble' and 'Dementia' and was a housekeeper in Virginia before she was deposited into the asylums growing census.

The staircase off the main lobby
Photo by author 2014

While researching this project, I found some very disturbing cases, not just at TALA in the early years, but also at asylums all over the country. In the early 1800's wives and daughters were often committed for not being obedient enough to their husbands or fathers. Women were expected to be homemakers and not much was given to their education. If a woman spoke out and went against the 'norm', she could be committed. I first became aware of this a couple of years ago. I was visiting a courthouse and noticed the term "lunacy" on many of the women's admission forms. Shockingly enough, a woman could be quite often divorced for reasons of lunacy. Her husband would put her in the asylum and then conveniently file for divorce. New wife, new life.

Men were committed for various reasons as well. This one chanced to be the very first male admission to TALA in 1864. He was the twelfth admission at the asylum and was admitted for melancholia and sunstroke. Sunstroke! He was just fifty-three years old. A thirty-eight year old merchant from Mason County was admitted later that year for "The War" and probably suffering from what we now know as Post Traumatic Stress Disorder. In the same year you have another male being admitted for masturbation at age twenty-eight in February of 1864. He was a cabinetmaker from Virginia and apparently had been spotted doing the 'evil act of masturbation', which caused his 'Acute Mania'. Many doctors and those in society as well, believed that alterations of blood flow during any sexual activity could lead to nerve damage, insanity, and blindness. An 18th Swiss physician named Tissot believed that masturbation was especially hazardous in this respect. An American physician of that era, Benjamin Rush, also viewed the practice of masturbation as dangerous to mental and physical health. He wrote several widely read articles on the subject. Even the man who initiated the Boy Scouts had his view. Lord Baden-Powell, founder of the Boy Scout movement stated that "if masturbation becomes a habit, it quickly destroys both health and spirits; he becomes feeble in body and mind and often ends in a lunatic asylum."

Admissions were often linked to sex, love and everything in between such as those with broken hearts. Another sad case at the asylum involved a broken heart *and* a spiritual medium, which was published in the Kansas City Star, dated March 26, 1899.

His Long Walk for Nothing.
A man's tramp from Missouri to Pennsylvania to Mary, and the finale.
From the Pittsburgh Dispatch.
Parkersburg, Pennsylvania

"During the blizzard a few weeks ago, a man of about 25 years of age, dressed as a cowboy, appeared at the police headquarters and asked for lodging. He claimed to be from Granby, Missouri from which place he had trudged on foot for the purpose of marrying a young girl named Ethel Darkwood. Ethel's home was in Upper Glades, Webster County, and she was said to be worth $25. The fellow gave his name is John Fairbee, and had tickets from a St. Louis matrimonial agency stating that he was a member of the Association and was authorized to marry Ms. Darkwood. He remained here overnight and started to walk the remaining 200 miles at the distance, refusing railroad transportation. A report reached here Saturday that he had been arrested and jailed at Addison in Webster County, as a lunatic. It developed that when he reached upper glades and found the woman, she was a widow with one child and in humble circumstances. As he was penniless, she refused to marry him and he lost his reason. When he passed through here, he carried a picture of a handsome country girl, who he said was his fiancée and stated that he had seen and conversed with her. It now seems that he saw and talked with the girl to the means of the spiritual medium, who also furnished him the photograph. He will be sent to the Weston Asylum for the Insane."

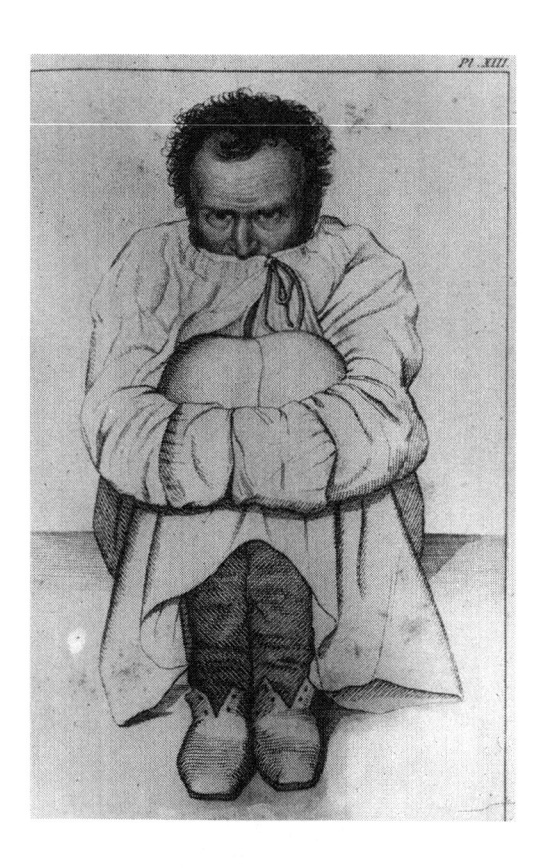

When children were committed, often times the families, probably due to embarrassment, would tell others they had died. Some children were committed for being an unwanted pregnancy, for disobedience or illness such as Down's syndrome or Autism. In as late as 1958, we have a stillborn being birthed at the hospital, only to end up buried in one of the hospital cemeteries that sit back behind the main hospital building. Little Crookshank baby was born on November 30th 1958 and went to be with the Lord. A much better place to be than the asylum, we would all agree. Little Henry Zink was only six years old when he died on July 13th 1929 from Spina Bifida. He is burial number #2338 in the cemetery record book compiled by Marlene Tenney, Joy Stalnaker and Hartzel Strader.

Reasons for Committal at TALA from 1864-1889
Amenorrhea
Bad company
Bad habits and political excitement
Bad whiskey
Bite of rattlesnake
Bloody flux
Brain fever
Business nerves
Carbonic acid gas
Carbuncle
Cerebral softening
Cold
Congestion of brain
Constitutional
Crime
Death of sons in war
Decoys into the Army
Deranged masturbation
Desertion by husband
Diphtheria
Disappointed affection
Disappointment
Disappointed love
Dissipation of nerves
Dissolute habits
Dog bite
Domestic affliction

Domestic trouble
Doubt about his mother's ancestors
Dropsy
Effusion on the brain
Egotism
Epileptic fits
Excessive sexual abuse
Excitement as officer
Explosion of a shell nearby
Exposure and hereditary
Exposure and quackery
Exposure an Army
Fall from a horse
False confinement
Feebleness of intellect
Fell from horse and war
Female disease
Fever and loss of lawsuit
Fever and nerved
Fever and jealousy
Fighting fire
Fits and desertion of husband
Gastritis
Gathering in the head
Greediness
Grief
Gunshot wound
Hard study
Hereditary predisposition
Hysteria
Ill-treated by husband
Imaginary phenyl trouble
Immoral life
Imprisonment
Indigestion
Intemperance
Intemperance and business trouble
Interference
Jealousy

Jealousy and religion
Kick of horse
Kicked in the head by a horse
Laziness
Liver and social disease
Loss of arm
Marriage of son
Masturbation and syphilis
Masturbation for 30 years
Medicine to prevent conception
Menstrual deranged
Mental excitement
Milk fever
Moral sanity
Novel reading
Nymphomania
Opium habit
Over action of the mind
Overheat
Over study of religion
Overtaxing mental powers
Parents were cousins
Pecuniary losses
Periodical fits, tobacco and masturbation
Political excitement
Politics
Puerperal
Religious enthusiasm
Religious excitement
Remorse
Rumor of husband murder
Salvation Army
Scarlatina
Seduction
Seduction and disappointment
Self-abuse
Severe labor
Sexual abuse and stimulants
Sexual derangement

Shooting of daughter
Smallpox
Snuff eating for two years
Softening of the brain
Spinal irritation
Suppressed masturbation
Suppression of menses
Sunstroke
Superstition
The War
Time of life
Trouble
Uterine derangement
Venereal excesses
Vicious vices in early life
Women trouble
Worms
Young lady in fear

My, oh my, how have things changed in this area of Psychiatry. A booklet published in 1989 spoke of the Involuntary Admission Procedure. We've come a long way baby!

<u>Weston Hospital Involuntary Admission Procedure</u>

1. Application is made to the Circuit court by an individual who has witnessed behavior indicating that the prospective patient has likely to cause harm to himself or others and the applicant believes that these behaviors are due to mental illness/retardation or addiction

2. The community mental health center is contacted and ordered to determine if alternative service is available that will prevent hospitalization.

3. The prospective patient is then examined and interviewed by a licensed psychiatric, psychologist or physician who determines if the person fits criteria for involuntary to a mental health facility

4 Once the certification (see #3) is completed, a mental health hearing is held in front of a magistrate, mental hygiene commissioner or circuit judge of the county of which the individual is a residence of has been found, The

individual must be present and represented by council.

5. Presiding judge/ mental hygiene commissioner/ magistrate will enter an order based on evidence presented as to whether probably cause has been found.

6. If probable cause has been found, then the individual will be transported to the designated mental health facility.

7. Within ten days of admission the physician of record will make a decision as to whether a final commitment application will be processed.

8. Recommendation for final commitment may be for a temporary observation period of up to 6 months or for an indeterminate period of commitment of up to 2 years. If a patient received either type of a commitment, it *does not* mean they will be in a mental health facility for that time but that the facility/patient will not necessarily have to return to court during that period of time.

9. If the physician decides not to make an application for commitment, then the client may be allowed to sign voluntary or will be discharged with appropriate planning.

In the 1980's there was a married couple who lived in the hospital in a small apartment area. They had AIDS and at that time, the health care system was not exactly sure how to handle cases such as this. In another case, there was an elderly man who had spent sixty years of his life in the asylum. When it closed in 1994, he did not want to leave. Asylum life was all that he had ever known and sadly, he had become institutionalized. What lay outside the asylum door was much more frightening to him than staying within its two foot thick stonewalls. This had been his home for sixty years. He was transferred out to another local facility, just as thousands of other patients were when the doors closed on that final day.

10
The White Plague Comes to Weston

Many a death at the asylum occurred because of tuberculosis, ominously referred to as the 'White Plague' or the 'White Death'. Tuberculosis was also listed as a condition known as phthisis, consumption, Potts Disease or even termed as the Wasting Disease. It caused the most widespread public concern in the 19th and early 20th centuries as an endemic disease of the urban poor. Early outbreaks in the United States were started by the drinking of unpasteurized cow milk. Poor living conditions, crowded environs, inclement weather and lack of sunlight are all contributing factors to the spread of this contagious disease. Physicians typically blamed both the poor themselves and their ramshackle-like houses and tent cities for the spread of the dreaded disease. People ignored public-health campaigns to limit the spread of contagious diseases, such as the prohibition of spitting on the streets, Health officials suggested mandatory quarantines, which separated families from TB stricken loved ones, but these were often ignored.

Tuberculosis was thought to be a hereditary disease initially, rather than a contagious one. In the days before medicine was available for the cure, treatments and experiments may have seemed barbaric. Patient's lungs were exposed to ultraviolet light to try to stop the spread of the bacteria.

Sunrooms were thought to be beneficial with this application of artificial light in place of sunlight. When the TB building was constructed at the asylum, open porches were used no matter if it what season. Fresh air was believed to be beneficial and a possible cure.

During this era of the outbreak, some of the populace regarded this as a romantic disease. The American poet, Henry David Thoreau, died from it along with Ralph Waldo Emerson's father. Edgar Allen Poe wrote about it due to the fact his wife perished as its victim. Many were accustomed to death in the Victorian era, as death was everywhere you looked. TB was feared, but regarded with a peculiar resignation because it was so unavoidable. It was dreaded, but at the same time romanticized. It was a disease that reflected the culture of its time. Picture the victim slowly and gracefully fading away, transcending their corporeal body, their immortal soul shining through and you think of a poem from Emily Dickenson. Even modern times have romanticized it somewhat as in Moulin Rouge and Les Misérables, for example.

In the 1920-30s, this disease was spreading so rapidly that a special building was used to house those with the ailment at TALA. In 1940, there was an influx of funds that the asylum had in its hands. The funds came to good use as a new building was constructed on the land to help isolate those stricken with tuberculosis. It typically attacks the lungs but can attack other parts of the body as well and the symptoms can manifest as fever, chills, night sweats, loss of appetite, weight loss, and fatigue. TB spreads very easily and quickly and if you have an overcrowded hospital, where patients are in close contact with each other and the staff and visitors, you have a big problem.

Some of the early deaths at the asylum listed 'consumption' as the cause of death as this was another name for TB. Poor Anna Adkins was 48 years old when she passed away on September 13 1920 from TB. She was a widow and was buried in one of the hospital cemeteries. Her grave is not marked. Thomas Arbogast suffered as Anna did. He died on July 24th 1947 and was just 29 when he succumbed to the White Plaque and ended up in one of the cemeteries on the hill behind the asylum.

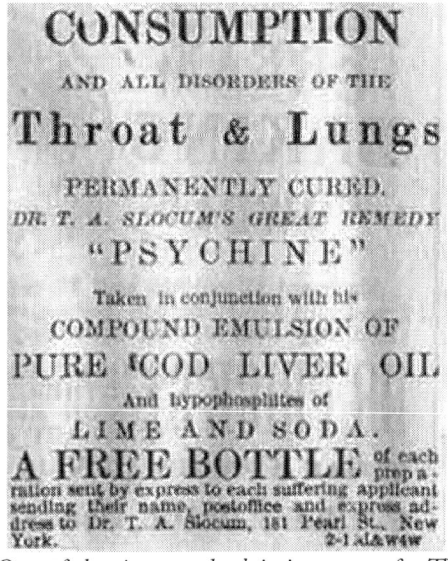

One of the vintage ads claiming a cure for TB

The disease is spread through the air with a simple cough or sneeze. It could spread from someone singing or even spitting. Some individuals who are infected do not have symptoms and this is known as latent tuberculosis. About one in ten latent infections eventually progresses to the active disease stage, which, if left untreated, kills more than 50% of those so infected.

When the new TB building was built in 1940, it was established on the southern end of the property far away from the main hospital. It was built to isolate those who were stricken with the disease. The medical approach to treating tuberculosis included extensive bed rest, exposure to fresh air and sunshine as discussed earlier, and a diet consisting of plenty of meat, fresh fruits, vegetables, and dairy products. The emphasis on fresh air and sunshine meant that the buildings site design and surrounding landscape were considered vital factors in the recovery of patients. It unfortunately, also helped spread the disease, which was airborne.

Blanket Weston X Rays Urged

The Charleston Gazette
The State Newspaper

Charleston, West Virginia, Saturday Morning, December 11, 1965 — 22 Pages—2 Sections—Ten Cents

By Thomas F. Stafford
Staff Writer

Atty. Gen. C. Donald Robertson recommended Friday that the services of the State Health Department's X-ray unit be offered to the entire population of Weston (8,754) as a result of the growing tuberculosis problem at Weston State Hospital.

Robertson's recommendation was contained in an opinion to Dr. N. H. Dyer, state health director, who had asked about the scope of his authority over mental institutions. Weston is the state's oldest and largest mental hospital.

Dyer said Friday free X rays will be offered to Weston's residents next week when patients and employes at Weston State Hospital are screened for tuberculosis.

The Weston hospital broke into the news earlier this week when it was discovered that there were more than 100 cases of tuberculosis there and they were not properly isolated from other patients and the staff.

Gov. Smith has since directed that the TB patients be transferred to Pinecrest Sanitarium at Beckley and everybody at the hospital — the 2,600 patients and staff — be tested by the health department's mobile X ray unit.

Robertson further suggested to Dr. Dyer that he check the visitor's register at the Weston institution and "notify all those who were possibly exposed" to consult their physician or county health officer so they can be examined.

"I make these suggestions not from a health standpoint," Robertson said. "Should any citizen, patient, visitor or otherwise contact tuberculosis as a result of negligence on the part of the state, then the state would be responsible and a claim for reimbursement would be justified."

At least, he added, such an examination would "quiet the emotional doubt" that a person might well experience as a result of having been exposed, as well as fear of contracting tuberculosis or transmitting it to his family.

Robertson's concern undoubtedly is the outgrowth of a letter from Dr. Cornelia B. Wilbur, Weston superintendent, in which she said the tuberculosis unit is a "flagrant health hazard for all of the employes and even the individuals in the town of Weston since our employes live in Weston."

DR. WILBUR'S Dec. 6 letter to Dr. Dyer, a confidential com-
(Please Turn to Page 2, Col. 2)

The TB building 2008
Photo by the author

This list is a compilation of the names I have come across in my research. Some names are taken from various newspaper clippings, obituaries and reference materials. It is by no means a complete list. Much credit is given to the "Cemeteries of Lewis County, WV and Adjacent Counties Volume XII", complied by Marlene Tenney, Joy Stalnaker and the late Hartzel Strader.

These patients are buried in unmarked graves in one of the hospital's cemeteries.

Sarah Ables died January 6, 1936 70 years old
Beulah Abrell died January 26 1925 21 years old
Anna Adkins died Sept 13 1920 48 years old
Minor Alkire died April 1 1907 26 years old
Charles Allen died November 3, 1924 61 years old
Florence Amos died October 10, 1904 29 years old
Thomas Arbogast died July 24, 1940 29 years old
Cecil Bailey died March 10, 1940 50 years old
John R Baker died March 2, 1919 80 years old

Tony Backus died January 2, 1960 85 years old
Charles Ball died March 15, 1898 unknown age
Frank Banks died January 17, 1904 30 years old
Marco Baric died September 8, 1930 51 years old
Lena Allen Barker died August 13, 1916 49 years old
Mary E Barlow died October 6, 1890 47 years old
Sophia Barton died November 5, 1893 40 years old
Arbie J. Bayes died September 4, 1955 55 years old
Harry Bee died April 22, 1938 39 years old
Jemima Bermen died October 8, 1898
Stephen J. Bird died December 24, 1896
Cecil Bishop died December 25 1960 49 years old
James Blume died March 24, 1947
Belva Bolen died September 27, 1950 47 years old
Anthony Boresky died April 10, 1940 56 years old
Effie Bowen died June 25, 1910 43 years old
Ida Bowen died August 24, 1912 44 years old
William M. Bowen died May 1819 73 years old
Jack Bradberry died August 30, 1940 29 years old
Barbara Bradshaw died June 16, 1898 85 years old
Mary Bratony died May 17 1943 31 years old
John Britton died April 21, 1912 26 years old
Asberry Brock died July 11 1898 75 years old
Dave Brown died July 13, 1920 324 years old
Frank Brown died March 24 1920 43 years old
Jane brown died December 4 1912 52 years old
John brown died December 23 1928 20 years old
John brown died December 19 1910 41 years old
Wanetta Brown died March 19, 1940 41 years old
William Brownlee died July 9, 1930 72 years old
Belle Buck died May 14, 1890 35 years old
Lizzie Buck died August 10, 1907 56 years old
Lulu Bundy died February 11, 1915 35 years old
Charles Bunner died June 25, 1920 24 years old
Robert Butler died September 16 1914 34 years old
Newton Caldwell died August 22 of 1914 45 years old
Marshall C Calvert died March 12, 1940 69 years old
Maria Camp died March 11, 1917 38 years old
Mary Camp died March 26, 1907 unknown age

Lina Campbell died May 30, 1940 41 years old
Goldie Canfield died April 9, 1948 32 years old
Emma L Carson died May 5, 1918 27 years old
Nancy Chaddock died April 11, 1940 39 years old
Hulda Chevorant died January 6, 1926 34 years old
Adam Clanahan died February 13, 1890 67 years old
Delpha Clayton died June 16, 1913 52 years old
Francine A. Clifton died April 5, 1890 49 years old
Jane Clifton died November 3, 1910 61 years old
Catherine Collier died March 12 1952
Henrietta Conderski died May 17, 1940 67 years old
Elijah Cooper died August 26, 1890 55 years old
Susan Cosner died May 25, 1933 37 years old
Dick Cotton died March 29, 1911 40 years old
Annie Cottrell died November 18, 1906 24 years old
Rosa Crim died March 29, 1927 51 years old
Sarah Culp died May 28, 1918 64 years old
Sarah E. Cunningham died June 16, 1930 78 years old
 Isabelle Curry died December 23, 1909 56 years old
Ella May Daily died December 2, 1930 50 years old
Flora Daugherty died September 28, 1930 38 years old
 Junior Davis died March 5, 1905 30 years old
Jeanette S Dixon died July 15, 1914 51 years old
Marvin L Dorsey died August 1, 1921 40 years old
Lockharr Duley died January 25, 1930 38 years old
Laura Duvall died June 5, 1920 648 years old
Carrie Eldridge died February 23, 1903 26 years old
Leland Ellis died December 30, 1940 18 years old
Tim Evans died January 9, 1955 60 years old
Chester W Eyler died March 21, 1922 32 years old
Loretta Fahner died April 22, 1930 40 years old
 Joe Farmville died December 15, 1912
Rosa Ferrell died April 2, 1918 40 years old
Emory Fielder died April 22, 1962 64 years old
Sallie Esta Fletcher died October 8, 1920 30 years old
Benjamin Flowers died May 6, 1893 unknown age
Lovie Franklin died May 20, 1914 43 years old
Alma Gaines died August 24, 1925 28 years old
Maggie Gainey died May 10, 1911 82 years old

LauraGawthrop died April 5, 1911 31 years old
Price Gaylor died May 3, 1930 25 years old
Pete George died April 18, 1947 31 years old
Frank Geretina died April 15, 1920 31 years old
Edward J Gill died August 3, 1907 64 years old
Spencer Gilmore died September 7, 1915 43 years old
John Glcum died February 2, 1897 unknown age
Alex Gluck died February 17, 1940 73 years old
Martha Grady died September 28, 1910 36 years old
Emma Graham died February 8, 1920 27 years old
Rosa Granato died July 13, 1924 19 years old
J. S. Grcily died September 29, 1890 52 years old
Lilllie Green died April 11, 1922 48 years old
Effie Anne Griffen died January 11, 1940 58 years old
Edna Magdalena Griffith died July 15, 1940 26 years old
Ida May Griffith died December 19, 1918 35 years old
Herbert Grogg died July 15, 1950 42 years old
Annie Guddel died December 8, 1880 35 years old
William Lee Gum died August 28, 1930 17 years old
Belle Hamilton died March 22, 1908 48 years old
Delphia Hanlin died November 24, 1923 50 years old
William C Harkness died January 11, 1960 39 years old
Noah Harmon died April 1, 1890 35 years old
Emma Harrison died July 9, 1910 59 years old
John Harrison died January 18, 1940 53 years old
Raymond Hart died March 16, 1930 20 years old
Charles Hartman died August 18, 1945 46 years old
Hannah Hawkenberry died June 18, 1903 28 years old
Annie M Hawkins died August 30, 1904 no age given
Henry Haywood died April 2, 1940 67 years old
Paul Henderson died July 2, 1960 57 years old
Melissa Hickman died January 14, 1905 38 years old
Clyde Hillman died March 19, 1940 33 years old
Tracy Hill died July 6, 1948 41 years old
John W Holly died February 29, 1892 20 years old
Kate Hooker died August 5, 1890 39 years old
Emma Hosaflock died January 12, 1940 39 years old
Ralph Hosaflock died September 15, 1932 23 years old
Martin Hosey died February 8, 1890 31 years old

John Hauser died June 30, 1896 35 years old
Friday Hosten and died January 16, 1918 38 years old
Mahala Howard died May 8, 1906 36 years old
Ada Hudnall died March 1, 1898 36 years old
Emory Hughes died November 14, 1922 55 years old
Maggie Irwin died April 17, 1962 39 years old
Harry Jarrell died July 5, 1938 31 years old
Dicie Jarvis died August 30, 1938 32 years old
George Johnson died February 8, 1906 53 years old
Eliza Jones died March 21, 1907 56 years old
Laura Jones died February 23, 1894 40 years old
George Kearns died December 20, 1913 24 years old
Paul Keenan died February 17, 1948 44 years old
Lizzie Keener died March 15, 1922 26 years old
Ottie Keith died August 30, 1950 78 years old
Emma Kelley died January 22, 1920 46 years old
Ina Keplinger died June 28, 1940 59 years old
Florence Kitte died June 13, 1906 20 years old
Jenny Knight died July 26, 1942 62 years old
Milka Koches died July 21, 1930 57 years old
Walter Korchum died January 7, 1940 46 years old
Addie Kriss died September 14, 1918 39 years old
George A. Langford died December 21, 1910 44 years old
Lewis Larke died December 20, 1890 57 years old
Clara Etta Lasure died December 27, 1930 39 years old
Jennie T. Lawrence died July 9, 1913 unknown age
Georgianna Lee died December 16, 1904 no age given
Rebecca Lee died May 17 of 1936 years old
Cosby Lefler died March 24, 1947 35 years old
Unknown Lewis died June 23, 1899 unknown age
Jacob Lidy died June 18, 1918 55 or 60 years old
Viola V. Liller died January 17, 1940 53 years old
James A. Lockwood died June 6, 1911 25 years old
Violet Loomis died July 27, 1955 54 years old
Jasper Louk died January 4 1945
Otis Lovegood died November 15, 1963 74 years old
Anna Belle Luderick died December 29, 1930 55 years old
Mary Lyle died April 5, 1930 62 years old
Alice Mace died August 16, 1940 40 years old

James Mahew died April 20, 1913 60 years old
Hattie Malcolm died March 8, 1945 58 years old
Emily Martin died March 25, 1919 27 years old
Julia Martin died December 11, 1919 50 years old
Wade Martin died June 2, 1929 about 15 years old
Raymond Mays died December 2, 1944 23 years old
Laura McComas died April 10, 1940 57 years old
John McDonald died July 20, 1917 48 years old
Jane McIe died April 18, 1917, 33 years old
Mary McVaney died Sept 17 1914 unknown age
Eugene Medberry died Nov 21, 1936 62 years old
Eliza Messengers died Feb 1915 unknown age
Frank Miahallis died Feb 15 1938 38 years old
Mary M Michaels died March 18, 1917 42 years old
Ellen Middleton died April 24, 1903 43 years old
Sallie Milam died September 23, 1931 78 years old
Mike Mile died January 19, 1920 47 years old
Mary Milum died April 5, 1913 52 years old
Nora Miner died February 14, 1905 30 years old
Otto Mitchell died August 9, 1950 73 years old
Pete Mitchell died March 12, 1940 39 years old
Lizzie Moats died February 11, 1911 30 years old
Roy Moats died August 20, 1930 36 years old
Katie Molnar died September 4, 1929 about 14 years old
Bascom Monroe died February 13, 1917 29 years old
Corbet J Monreo died December 18, 1937 30 years old
John Monroe died September 2, 1914 56 years old
Walter Moore died February 24, 1924 33 years old
Ettie Morris died March 26, 1920 34 years old
Ted Clayton Morrison died December 27, 1961 59 years old
Gauryl Mruz died July 24, 1919 29 years old
Lucy G Muncey died Dec 25 1912 34 years old
Cecil Myers died November 8, 1910 unknown age
Louis E Myers died April 5, 1903 53 years old
Walter Clifford Neal died May 10, 1940 29 years old
Lewis Neff died April 19, 1930 17 years old
Joseph Nidichi died December 11, 1930 50 years old
Matt Oreskovich died November 21, 1920 35 years old
Lisa Osborne Patton died January 13, 1917 33 years old

Mary Peyton died August 25, 1903 34 years old
Lillie Peck died August 6, 1918 49 years old
Andy Penasky died September 2, 1840 51 years old
Blanche Phillips died November 12, 1930 51 years old
Francis Phillips died April 22, 1922 about 40 years old
Charles Porter Piggott died September 28, 1938 30 years old
David Plate died January 23, 1896 27 years old
Warren Posey died October 3, 1940 24 years old
Enoch Price died June 30, 1930, 29 years old
Stella Prunty died March 26, 1908 32 years old
Katie Przyoova died April 6, 1930 37 years old
Ruhama Pullam died February 23, 1930 66 years old
Walter Rader died November 26, 1933 51 years old
Robert Reed died February 25, 1930 47 years old
Ethel Reinhard died February 12, 1938 59 years old
Glenn Edwards Reynolds died December 15, 1945 21 years old
James Reynolds died May 19, 1948 age 24
Mary Hilda Reynolds died January 18, 1948 20 years old
Cloyd Ridenour died October 5, 1930 19 years old
Charles Roberts died August 14, 1948 26 years old
Katie Roderick died January 13, 1930 33 years old
Andrew Rollyson died July 7, 1890 46 years old
Myrtle Roman died June 7, 1918 40 years old
Katie Ross died May 23, 1919 unknown age
Sarah Runyon died March 27, 1940 71 years old
Anna Teresa Sarsfiled died October 24, 1940 40 years old
Texie Saunders died April 13, 1898 22 years old
Michael Saxton died November 1, 1907 unknown age
Mrs. Dora Schmidt he October 14, 1893 61 years old
Ida Scholobohm died April 20, 1930 44 years old
Lucy J Schoolcraft died July 25, 1930 32 years old
Mary J Schoolcraft died October 19, 1930 33 years old
Percy Scott died April 3, 1918 23 years old
Henrietta P Shelby died June 1900 39 years old
Willa Shepard died June 13, 1920 27 years old
James Shreves died March 14, 1890 19 years old
Ella Sidwell died April 10, 1916 about 21 years old
Frank Simcis this November 7, 1917 43 years old
Margaret A Simmons died April 9, 1892 33 years old

A J Smith died May 24, 1890 24 years old
Mary Smith died February 10, 1920 56 years old
William E Snyder died October 29, 1930 46 years old
William H Sprigg died august 21 1931 47 years old
Emma Stealey died February 7, 1903 31 years old
James Stevens died September 22, 1880 39 years old
Emery Stier died December 12, 1932 34 years old
Margaret Stipp died April 28, 1911
Etta Stovall died July 13, 1910 26 years old
Sis Stovall died October 25, 1913 32 years old
William G Stricklin died September 18, 1917 57 years old
John Struthers died June 19, 1926 43 years old
Viola Summers died May 17, 1932 23 years old
Albert Suoaks died December 23, 1936 57 years old
Lakah Belle Sutton died September 8, 1960 72 years old
Mila Svetech died September 3, 1931 53 years old
James A Tabor died June 26, 1943 51 years old
Rose Taylor died April 27, 1935 30 years old
Henry Theiss died January 1, 1939 73 years old
Sallie Thomas died November 15, 1920 15 years old
Luther Thomas died July 9, 1919 31 years old
Arthur Lee Thurmond died February 8, 1929 17 years old
Cora Tillenghurst died May 3, 1892 27 years old
Victor Tisch died June 27, 1930 42 years old
Hattie Twyman died June 25 1913 40 years old
Delta Ure died January 27 1910 33 years old
Rebecca Vanscoy died August 23, 1910 54 years old
Hazel Vargo died December 23, 1933 40 years old
Robert Wade died December 3, 1890 41 years old
Sarah Wade died July 27, 1907 53 years old
Virgi E Ware died April 1, 1934 28 years old
William C Watkins died December 22, 1918 50 years old
Arthur Waugh died October 17, 1907 unknown age
Lloyd Waugh died June 2, 1940 56 years old
Mary Weimer died July 2, 1902 unknown age
Maggie Welt died February 5, 1914 31 years old
Mrs. Sidney West died May 20, 1917 46 years old
Nathaniel West died June 12, 1922 unknown age
Annie Wetzel died July 3, 1912 unknown age

John Whalen died March 28, 1903 40 years old
Mary Whitney died November 4, 1890 56 years old
Lulu Widner died March 11, 1930 41 years old
Lewis Wetzel Wilfong died August 13, 1955 56 years old
Susan Wilfong died March 22, 1907 55 years old
Anna E Wilson died May 2, 1907 69 years old
Nevada Coplfox Wilson died August 19, 1930 73 years old
Walter Woods died May 22, 1930 21 years old
Columbus Wright died June 19, 1889 29 years old
John Zaboronski died April 23, 1940 66 years old

> Spitting is **DANGEROUS** and **ILLEGAL!** **TUBERCULOSIS** is transmitted in this way and kills more people than any other disease.

Thomas F. Stafford's
AFFAIRS OF STATE

Weston Problem Beyond 'Routine'

The tuberculosis scare at Weston State Hospital illustrates quite adequately the devices some officials will use to tranquilize public opinion when their own or the derelictions of their subordinates are given the bright light of publicity.

From several points came angry denials that an "epidemic" existed at Weston, as if this changed the basic facts of the case. They used this one word as their peg in trying to return the reading and listening public to the viewpoint that all is sweetness and light at West Virginia's largest mental hospital.

The word "epidemic" is one that newsmen and doctors have differed over as to its meaning since the days of typhoid f e v e r and diphtheria when a localized outbreak of a communicable disease sent people for miles around into a frenzy of inner torment and fear.

INTERCEPTED MESSAGE

Dec. 11, 1965

Dear Arthur:
 Cynics and Republicans might say there are plenty of suspects.

Yours,

George

C. A. Blankenship,
Seal Searcher,
City.

(Story on Page 13)

Doctors were at a loss as to how to cure TB early on, but there were a few treatments that were thought to help or slow down the disease. As the century progressed, some surgical interventions (including the pneumothorax technique where meant surgeons would collapse an infected lung to "rest" it and allow the lesions to heal) were used to treat the disease.

A desperate sounding attempt to cure TB was announced when doctors proclaimed to the newspapers that "the so called ice pick operation is the best treatment for mental patients with tuberculosis." Three doctors at the asylum wrote an article in the American Journal of Psychiatry stating that the three-minute procedure helped patients sleep and eat better. In this way, they would be able to bring the tuberculosis under control. It sounded incredulous to me. The author of the article were Dr. Sylvia Cheng, head of the TB unit, Dr. H. Sinclair Tait and of course, Dr. Lobotomy himself, Walter Freeman. At the time of the article, it was noted that fifty-seven patients had been treated and the results were found to be "gratifying." Further stating, "The operation takes less than three minutes and recovery is prompt, and the patient is often ready for their next meal." I am not sure what kind of a response I had after reading the entire column. It was somewhere between shock and repulsion.

The first genuine success in immunizing against tuberculosis was developed from attenuated bovine-strain tuberculosis by Albert Calmette and Camille Guérin in 1906. It was called "BCG". The BCG vaccine was first used on humans in 1921 in France, but it was not until after World War II that BCG received widespread acceptance in the United States, Great Britain, and Germany. The real cure came in 1944 when Albert Schatz, Elizabeth Bugie, and Selman Waksman streptomycin, the first antibiotic and first bacterial agent effective against the White Plague.

11
Scandal, Fire, & Escape

Any large institution will eventually have a scandal or two darken its past. This was also true of the asylum. In 1899 a story broke in many newspapers both local and in other states and caused shock and dismay among family members, dedicated staff and the general public. The Weston State Hospital Investigation was covered in the Weston Democrat and played out like a torrid novelette. Dr. Strathers, the current superintendent at the asylum, was being charged with questionable conduct with female patients. He had six children with his wife and was of good standing at the hospital but apparently and by some accounts and testimony, was allegedly a ladies man. He was found *not guilty* of the crimes stated although there were witnesses. The local newspapers suggested a "whitewash" and public opinion varied. The order read:

"On motion, it is ordered that the board proceed to consider the charges filed against the Superintendent, and all evidence presented in connection therewith, and after mature consideration the board is of the opinion that the prosecution has failed to sustain the charges so filed against said W. E. Strathers, Superintendent, and find him not guilty as charged."

Regardless, a new Superintendent replaced him within one year. Dr. A. H. Kunst took the reins as the head of the asylum. It took a while before the flames of this scandal quieted down.

A couple of decades later and after the Strathers scandal smoldered out, a much more real fire erupted at the asylum. After the central section of the main hospital building was completed in the year 1871, Superintendent Thomas Camden had expressed grave concern of the possibility of a fire breaking out and wreaking havoc. Loss of life and damage to the buildings could be catastrophic. The problem was that patients had plenty of time to hatch plans and recruit helpers. Patients could be very creative and finding some combustibles in the size of a building like the asylum could be an easy task for someone who was a lover of fire. If a fire were to break out, Camden thought great destruction and loss of life would commence.

There had been small fires reported throughout the years but it was not until 1935 that the big one happened. It began on Thursday October the 3rd when it was noticed on the fourth floor. The next day, The Charleston Daily Mail stated that Marsh sounded the dinner gong and that all of the men, as they did every day, marched into the dining hall expecting a meal. No patient was harmed but one man barely escaped. This patient had been sleeping when the bell was rung and woke a few minutes later to find himself surrounded by flames. Two firefighters put a 55-foot ladder against the building, and the fire chief bravely climbed up to rescue the lucky man. All patient rooms have iron bars over the windows to prevent escape. This man who was to be rescued, summoned great strength and with his bare hands, bent the bars wide enough to escape. He was then helped to the ground.

PYROMANIAC IS SOUGHT

Attempts Made To Fire West Virginia Insane Hospital.

The Morning Herald Oct 29 1935

After the fire was out, many patients no longer had a ward that was livable so they staff set about securing a location for the displaced to stay. Around three hundred patients were transferred to Jackson's Mill, which is a local 4-H camp. The total in the ward was around three hundred and ninety but about eighty- ninety were able to stay at the hospital. They were all able to and return to the asylum once the wards were repaired.

The damage was estimated between $150,000 and $200,000. Firefighters came on scene from Weston, Buckhannon and Clarksburg to help quell the flames. The wing of the men's section actually collapsed leaving just the massive stonewalls standing tall. Unbelievably, there was no insurance on the building. What was the cause of the destruction? Deputy Marshal Berry believed it was started from defective electrical wiring but this was later proven wrong. The state needed funds to rebuild the institution so they applied for WPA (Works Program Administration) appropriation funds to help rebuild the portion of the hospital that was damaged. President Roosevelt authorized $115,000 in funds to help with the re building of the wing. The cause of the fire was blamed on an 18-year-old male who confessed that he started the fire in an empty room just below the clock tower. His name was Forrest Culver. A newspaper in Hagerstown, Maryland had this to say about the event. "Forrest Culver, age eighteen of Richmond Virginia, who has been at the asylum for the last six years, is now being held in solitary confinement." Taken from the Morning Herald October 29, 1935.

October 4th 1935
Charleston Daily Mail newspaper showing the fire of 1935

Several days after the big fire, another one was begun. It wasn't as serious as the last one but officials had a feeling it was arson. Overall, there were six fires within a few months. Observant staff put all of the smaller fires out. No casualties were reported. Things quieted down....until November 29th. Bloodhounds were set lose after another fire broke out. They traced a patient back into the hospital and led the officials to sixteen year old Earl James Lloyd. He has been a patient of the asylum since age 12. After some initial denial, he confessed to starting all seven fires. He admitted that he had somehow acquired the keys to the entire south wing and had access to what areas and supplies he needed. He told authorities he lit the fires because of the "thrill and excitement."

Boy Takes All Blame For Starting Fires In Weston Hospital

A 17-year-old feeble-minded boy received and took all blame today for starting seven fires at the Weston state hospital with a loss of between $40,000 and $50,000.

Earl James Lloyd, of New Cumberland, who became a patient at the institution for the insane in 1931, grinned as he told Fire Marshal Fred B. Watkins he set the blazes over a period of three months "to see the fires and the engines run."

The accepted confession was Lloyd's second. On November 23—after bloodhounds followed a scent from the site of the latest fire to his cot—he told Watkins he started the blazes because three men paid him $10 a fire.

Changed His Story

Watkins asserted Lloyd changed his story. After two weeks of intermittent questioning the fire marshal said the boy admitted no others were involved.

The marshal, who directed Lloyd be locked in his room at the institution, said:

"The boy has a remarkable memory. He told us exactly how he started each of the fires, the date and time, and his memory jibbed with our records.

"He undoubtedly is a pyromaniac. He told us he got the idea for the fires from an accidental blaze earlier in the summer.

"I am convinced the case is solved but we still are taking every precaution at the hospital to see that none of the other patients are fire-minded."

Charleston Gazette December 14 1935

Pyromaniacs were not the only cause of concern for the staff and superintendent. The patient census in 1938 was high with 1,661 souls being housed. In the very same year, a survey was initiated by a Dr. Jones Granville who conducted it through the Survey of Mental Hospital Committee. It did not shed a positive and complimentary light on the institution. He wrote that in the center portion of the main hospital building there were administration offices, a small amount of bedrooms, the dining rooms and kitchen. There were two wings, the south one was for the men, and the north one was used for the women. These wards were very long with rooms on both sides and a large sitting room central for day activities. A few walls had recently been painted and there were curtains in place to brighten up the atmosphere. In some of the rooms, there were wooden chairs or benches and some metal beds. Many rooms had only a cot and no bed at all. The survey was the "beginning of consideration being given to closing the 88 year old hospital for a more modern, state of the art facility." The Survey continued with the fact that they "found that the hospital housed "epileptics, alcoholics, drug addicts and non-educable mental defectives" among its population. A series of newspaper articles by The Charleston Gazette in 1949, found poor sanitation, dim lighting, unsuitable furniture and heating in much of the complex. It was the first official suggestion of a possible closing.

> Dr. Charles Zeller, superintendent since May 1949, acknowledged that the sprawling institution still was tragically overcrowded.
>
> Dr. Zeller reported a total population of 1,981. This compared with slightly more than 1,800 in the early part of 1949.

Another study was done and this was another death knell for the asylum. Mrs. Charles Hoag from St Albans WV stated that the hospital was "sprawling over a quiet expanse of well-tended lawns, (which) conceals behind its imposing facades the worst and the best of West Virginia's care for the mentally ill." According to Mrs. Hoag, the southern wing, where the fire had been, was cheery, and was the "best of West Virginia's care." The northern wing however, which had not been redone, was the "worst."

> With all the improvements, however, Weston still earns its years old reputation of being —"the worst and the best in the care of mentally ill in West Virginia."

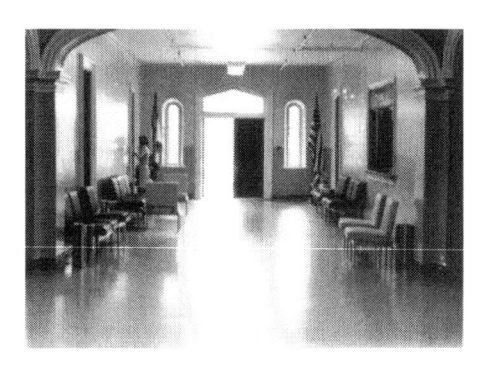

The hospital was overflowing with patients by 1949, according to a report filed by Mrs. Hoag. She reported that more than 1,800 were crammed into "long, dreary dormitories" and in "miserable, depreciated quarters which could never pass minimum inspection standards for domestic animals." Seeing that the hospital was severely overcrowded and in poor condition, renovations were underway by 1951 with a visit from Senator Robert Byrd who noted the improvements being made in the structure. Nevertheless, the overcrowding was progressively getting worse. By this time, 2,400 patients were crowded into a facility meant to house just 250. The superintendent at the time heartily agreed. Superintendent Knapp noted the deplorable conditions and pulled no punches in showing the reporters around the asylum. He noted that the lawns and grounds were beautiful but there was not enough staff to ensure that patients had time outdoors. Sleeping areas were overcrowded with thirty-nine beds in an area meant for only twenty allowed sufficient room to walk between them safely. The ceiling above rotting away as toilets on the floor above leaked incessantly. Heat is at a minimum as heating pipes had corroded. Windowpanes rattled with the slightest of breeze making it very uncomfortable in the winter.

Inmates at Weston Have to Live In Quarters Unfit for Livestock

Two elderly inmates of Weston State hospital are shown above performing dish washing chores in ordinary laundry tubs after a meal with their fellow patients. This unsanitary condition, the battered tin drinking cups, cramped quarters and inadequate facilities point up the lack of simple necessities to care for the state's mentally ill.
(Gazette Photo by Frank Wilkin)

January 24th, 1949 Charleston, West Virginia Daily Gazette

Knapp commented that the asylums farm animals received better care than most of the patients. To prove his point he mentions the women suffering from incontinent and how they sat scantily clad in their own excrement for many hours at a time. They were a special problem on the wards for the severely disturbed, as were the males suffering from the same condition. Only two staff member were on duty for fifty-two women "whose minds were beyond repair. They sway to and fro in archaic rocking chairs, roam incessantly up and down the floors and sit in that foul-smelling cell which by no stretch of imagination could ever be connected with the respectful description of a hospital." The January 24th 1949 Daily Gazette brought to light the dark needs of a hospital outgrowing itself and its original goal.

Considering the dismal outlook for one committed, it is no surprise that escapes occurred. Some patients who could function and be considered harmless would be allowed leave on certain weekends. They would wander into Weston and get a cup of coffee or walk the streets. Come Sunday, they headed back to the asylum. The only home any of them had ever known. The asylum provided the basic needs: a bed, food and protection from society and the elements.

Escapes occurred and had since the early days when those nine men escaped in 1867 during the early construction phase. In May of 1958, a convicted slayer by the name of Ivan Hoover was still at large. Ivan had been committed to the asylum in October the year before after killing his parents with a mattock at their home in Ricthie County. He was walking in a 'secure' area when he suddenly climbed a fence and took off running. They believed him to be shoeless and the newspaper alerted folks to be on the lookout for a six-foot tall, 170 pound man with brown hair, brown eyes and no shoes. He was captured about two weeks later only ten miles from Weston. Two farmers held him at gunpoint until law officials arrived and escorted him back to the asylum in a truck. He promptly fell asleep in the truck after stating he had not had a bite to eat and had been hiding out in the woods since leaving the asylum.

12
The Closing of the Hospital

The hospital would be listed in the National Register of Historic Places on April 19th of 1978 but that would not stop it from being closed by the state of West Virginia. New treatments in mental health care brought about a dramatic reduction in patients by the 1980's. In 1986, West Virginia Governor Arch Moore announced plans to build a new psychiatric facility elsewhere in the state and was considering converting the Weston Hospital to a prison. Ultimately, the new facility, the William R. Sharpe Jr. Hospital, was built in Weston and the old Weston State Hospital was simply closed in May 1994. The proposed plan by Moore failed to come to fruition and it was not converted into a prison. (Thankfully.)

Reports of bad conditions and overcrowding plagued the asylum for many years and it was no secret. In as recent as 1985, a Charleston newspaper stated "Weston Hospital is dirty and unkept" with patients "confined to dirty wards with bathrooms smeared with feces." Murders and suicides continued to be reported casting an even greater shadow on the building and its staff. In 1992, a patient was finally found after going missing. His decomposing body was found eight long days later. It was reported that they thought it was to be ruled a suicide.

In 1994, the state moved the patients out of the asylum and into their new home at the William Sharpe Hospital. In 1999, several city and county police officers playing paintball damaged all four floors of the interior of the main building. It would stand empty for a total of 15 years until a determined man with a vision would purchase the monstrous building.

The hospital graces the files of the National Historic Landmark program with its Statement of Significance being designated on June 21, 1990. Prior to its closing. The Statement of Significance reads as this:

One of the largest hand cut stone masonry buildings in America, the Weston Hospital took two decades to build following the original 1858 plan. Beautifully preserved tis his West Virginia facility, once quite isolated, was also self-sufficient and was a model architectural community that operated successfully for over 100 years. It is also one of a small number of 19th-century institutions that survives the United States to illustrate the great reforms in the treatment of mental illness.

Condition;
This landmark has been vacant since 1994 when the hospital facilities were transferred to a new building. Currently there is no reuse or long-term preservation plan for the structure, although the State, the Lewis County economic development Authority and the Weston historic landmarks commission are now investigating alternative compatible new uses in the past few years, some stabilization work is been carried out on the deteriorating structure, and the state now provides 24 hour security and grounds maintenance services. In addition, three cemetery sites were cleared and a better access road through the farm provided for the public. However, the state lacks an adequate maintenance budget address costlier problems like the deteriorating sandstone. Funding for the rehabilitation the building was appropriated to the save America's treasures grant program and the state is in process of acquiring a match. The building is still vacant.

In 2007, the West Virginia Department of Health and Human Resources auctioned the hospital and on August 29 of that year, its new owner took over. Mr. Joe Jordan purchased the building and remaining land for 1.5 million with initial active bidding starting at $500,000. He soon opened the asylum front doors to tours and other money raising events for its expensive and seemingly unending restoration. As the doors closed, another new chapter in the asylum's history had begun.

Newspaper photo showing the Old Soldiers Ward (Civil War section)

Photo by author 2014

13
Ghosts, Spirits, & Shadows

"True love is like ghosts, which everyone talks about and few have seen."
Francois de La Rochefoucauld

I am a paranormal investigator and a researcher. History is my passion and for that I have been called a para-historian and I think that suits me just fine. I like the darker side of history and for whatever reason, I gravitate to it. How did I get to be this way?

I cut my teeth on some of those wild, imaginative shows that were on television back in the late 60's and 70's. *The Twilight Zone* and *the Outer Limits* were my choices for evening shows on television. When I learned to read, some of my favorite books would soon be a tip off to what lay ahead in my life. Books on subjects such as UFOs, extra sensory perception, aliens, spiritualism, folklore, angels and the Salem Witchcraft Trials, would all be checked out on my little library card. I am sure the librarians wondered. I soon discovered the classic monster movies such as the old Universal Studios, *Dracula* and *Frankenstein*. They are still some of my all-time favorites. Dressing up for Halloween was always fun, of course. I relished autumn and the arrival of Halloween and it soon became my favorite holiday. In sixth grade, I played the wicked witch in the *Snow White and the Seven Dwarfs* play in grade school. I guess it was my destiny to start reading and researching haunted locations when I was a teen. In my early 20's I went on my first "ghost hunt". Friends of mine invited me to go explore an old abandoned house in the woods just over the county line from where I lived. Nothing happened of course, other than the multitude of mosquito bites you would expect on a hot summer night. That and the fact none of us had a flashlight…or permission to be on that property. My, oh how things have changed. I always have a flashlight (and extras) and I always get permission!

I am often asked if a certain location is haunted. People ask me that quite often. If you are familiar with the history of the asylum, I do not have to tell you that TALA is a place where paranormal activity has happened and still occurs. You don't have to believe me. All you have to do is visit TALA for yourself and decide. There is a room on the first floor of the asylum, which is called the "Paranormal Room". It has a sign above the door. Step inside that room and read some of the documents on the wall. Take some time to look through the Paranormal Reports file and read a few of the voluntary reports submitted from tourists and ghost hunters from all over the world. You will soon realize that hundreds, if not thousands of people have all experienced *something* paranormal here. Whether it is capturing an orb in a photo or perhaps seeing the image of a shadow person while strolling the hallways…it has happened repeatedly.

If you missed this big AP announcement back in May of 2008, here it is again.

WESTON HOSPITAL OFFICIALLY HAUNTED, GHOST HUNTERS DECLARES

The famed Sci Fi Channel "Ghost Hunters" has declared West Virginia's most famous mental hospital haunted. Jason Hawes and Grant Wilson of the Trans-Atlantic Paranormal Society visited the Lunatic Asylum West of the Alleghenies in March to try to debunk reports of unusual activity. People have said that they had heard gurneys moving up and down the hallways and screams from inside the former shock therapy room. Using hi tech-recording equipment, TAPS (Trans-Atlantic Paranormal Society) recorded what sounded like female laughter and a voice that said, "Go home." Wilson also saw a shadow that looked like it was holding its hands over its head and crouching before "being sucked out of the room."

While Jason and Grant were filming for their television series, they had a few experiences. They saw light at the end of the hallway and shortly afterwards they heard a voice in between them. Several staff members claimed that they had recognized the voice as a former patient known as old Ruth. She was a patient in Ward C where the most violent female patients were held. She was transferred to Ward 1 (on the first floor) after injuring herself. While sitting in the hallway, she was often confined to a feeding chair. Old Ruth would yell at people passing by saying, "Go home, damn you!"

Tour guides on the evening ghost hunt at TALA are often asked where the most haunted area is in the building. Answers vary but almost every section, ward, and hallway of the asylum has had something unusual happen. Whether it is the typical (and controversial) orb appearing in photographs, to personal experiences. People have had their hair pulled, been touched on the hand, leg, arm or back and a multitude of other experiences. Multiple voices have been captured on tape/digital and cassette. These voices are thought to be from beyond our realm. Ghost voices or spirit voices are believed to be able to be recorded and played back. They are out of the auditory range of humans- like a dog whistle. When you play the tape back, you can hear the voice. It's the same way with a dog whistle. We cannot hear it but a dog certainly can. Blow a dog whistle and record it. Play it back and supposedly, you can hear it. EVP (Electronic Voice Phenomena is mentioned throughout this chapter as an experience of many paranormal investigators.

Photo by the author 2014

My haunted history tours have given me the ability to take several hundred people into the facility for an overnight investigation. These night investigations usually start about 9:00 pm with a tour and then free time to explore on your own until about 5 am. Most everyone stays until 5 am. This building is not only one of the most fascinating to me, but one of our favorites to explore. If you are interested in attending one of our events at TALA, be sure to check out our website as www.HauntedHistory.net

The glory of holding my own events is that I get a great deal of people who return repeatedly. It is like one big, happy haunted family. They love the buildings and the chance to explore them overnight and at your own pace, is a great thing. Unless, of course, you have something really weird happen. Such is the case with **Dale from Pennsylvania**. Dale has been on multiple events with me since 2005 when he went to the West Virginia Penitentiary with me for an overnight hunt. He came on the very first TALA overnighter that I held back in 2011. He never came back on another event after that one. Why? Read what he had to say.

"It was a place I had been wanting to visit since I first heard about it in 2008. The hunt was much anticipated by my wife and I and we had taken off that Friday thru Tuesday so that we could enjoy the Weston area. Sherri's ghost hunt was that weekend and we had bought lots of new equipment to use. I never got to use anything but my camera though. I was standing in one of the old Doctors apartments and had been looking out the window at the sky. It was a full moon and I thought how neat it was that we were there on a full moon. I turned around to talk to my wife, but she had wandered into the next room without me noticing. As I started to take a step toward the darkened hallway, I heard a sound off to my right. It started me enough that I almost dropped my camera. As I swung my flashlight into the corner, this sounds crazy I know…but I saw a man. He was there for just seconds but he was just as solid as he could be. He had on a weird type of dress though….almost like a long nightgown but he was definitely male. I hurried through the doorway towards my wife and the safety of another room. The room I left just felt, well, it felt kind of bad. Like I was not welcome there. I have never experienced anything like that before and it really took the fun out of the night for me. I loved the building. The tour guide was great. Sherri was a super host but man, I never want to feel that way again. We left early. Really early. Like before midnight early. Thanks for a great time but we plan on doing our ghost hunting in a place not so big and dark!"

Photo by the author 2014

Karla H. from Kentucky came along on the same night and brought her two girlfriends. They told me later that they smelled some foul odor as they walked thru the Civil War area. Karen's friend is a bit of a sensitive and she felt that they were in the presence of a Civil War soldier who had some kind of a foot wound. The smell came over them quickly, and left just as fast.

After the August 2014 overnight event with Haunted Heartland Tours, **Jamie Umlauf** filled me in on something that happened to her while investigating that evening. This is her story in her own words. "I was at the TALA ghost hunt on Saturday with Denise Ciresi, Sarah Martin and Lance Tipton from Spirit Rising Paranormal. I wanted to share one of the experiences I had there and wanted to see if there had been any other reports of this happening. I smelled horses in the Civil War room when we were taking the quick tour at the beginning of the night. It was as if I was standing next to a horse. Actually, as soon as I smelled it I pictured two big horses, one in front of me and one next to me. It wasn't the manure smell, it was the actual smell of the horse itself. I have been around horses a lot in my life and it actually a smell that always makes me smile and brings back really great memories. The smell seemed to linger for a few seconds, but as soon as I turned around it was gone and I couldn't smell it anymore. I saw the buggies behind me and just brushed it off and told myself the smell could be from the buggies...even though I knew better. I told Denise about it and we both forgot until we read the sign in front of the building. It said that horses were occasionally housed in the building when needed and the rest of the building had not been built yet. We both just stared at each other in disbelief when we read that. I think smelling the horses at the beginning like that eased my nerves a bit. I was getting slightly uncomfortable as we walked through during the tour and after I smelled the horses, I wasn't afraid anymore. Has anyone ever experienced anything like that before? I wanted to put it in the evidence book that was in the paranormal room, but I had forgotten about it until the next day. In addition, I noticed a difference in feeling/energy when we went up to the top floor where the drug addicts and alcoholics were housed. The other wards just seemed like empty chaos if that makes any sense, but the top floor felt calm and very sad. I felt really depressed when we sat up there for a while. It was as if maybe the spirits that lingered there were embarrassed and depressed and that's why they wouldn't come out of the rooms for us. We started getting very mild activity from the end of the drug addiction ward. It sounded like possible footsteps. As if someone was slowly moving around in their room. I noticed that the activity started up once we changed the way we spoke to the spirits. It was as if they became more comfortable with us and maybe almost trusted us a little. As soon as others began walking around and making a lot of noise, the activity stopped."

Lance Tipton, Sarah Root Martin, Jamie Umlauf and Denise Ciresi attending the TALA ghost hunt with Haunted Heartland Tours on August 30th of 2014. Lance had this to say about his night; "Sarah and I had awesome experience with tour guide, Paul, at the Alcohol Ward with our flashlights going on and off on command. Sarah, Paul and I got very cold!" Lance, Sarah, Jamie and Denise are part of Spirit Rising Paranormal from Ohio. Case member Terry Pennington submitted the formal Case Report to the groups files. The report noted a waxing quarter moon with evidence submitted as positive for EVP's and temperature changes. Personal experiences were noted.

After a review of the digital recordings by Patti Martynowski (SRP Founder) and Terry Pennington (SRP Tech) there were a number of EVPs captured by Jamie and Denise while investigating. Below is what was heard after a review of the evidence.

    1.   EVP 1 (Living quarters for staff) Denise and Jamie were discussing the size of the rooms when an EVP came over saying "it's small".

    2.   EVP 2 (Ward R? we were lost) This EVP was especially interesting because not only was it caught on the recorder but also both Denise and Jamie heard a voice say something. This created a small humorous exchange between the two with Jamie saying the Denise talked and Denise insisting that it was not her. Denise first asked if Jamie heard a man's voice and then Jamie started telling Denise it was she. The EVP

captured was isolated and what the two heard was real. It was a man's voice saying, "Get out now". This was probably the best EVP of the night for these two.

3. EVP 3 (location unknown) This EVP was captured as Denise and Jamie were going between the rooms. Denise was worried that one of the doors would close and latch on them so she was trying to put a camera strap in it to hold it when a voice (male) was captured saying "Is that George".

4. EVP 4 (location unknown) Denise and Jamie were exploring one of the hallways when Denise thought she saw something down the corridor. She asked Jamie but neither could actually see what it was…The recording picked up what sounds like an old man wheezing like he was having a hard time breathing.

Overall, the night was successful for Team Spirit Rising. They had some exciting encounters and some great evidence that they brought home.

Denise Ciresi joined in with an overnight investigation in 2014. This is their account in her own own words; "After the August 2014 overnight event with Haunted Heartland Tours, Jamie Umlauf filled me in on something that happened to her while investigating that evening. "I was at TALA with Denise Ciresi from Spirit Rising Paranormal. I wanted to share one of the experiences I had there and wanted to see if there had been any other reports of this happening. I smelled horses in the Civil War room when we were taking the quick tour at the beginning of the night. It was as if I was standing next to a horse. Actually, as soon as I smelled it I pictured two big horses, one in front of me, and one next to me. It was not the manure smell; it was the actual smell of the horse itself. I have been around horses a lot in my life and it actually a smell that always makes me smile and brings back great memories. The smell seemed to linger for a few seconds, but as soon as I turned around it was gone and I could not smell it anymore. I saw the buggies behind me and just brushed it off and told myself the smell could be from the buggies…even though I knew better. I told Denise about it and we both forgot until we read the sign in front of the building. It said that horses were occasionally housed in the building when needed and the rest of the building had not been built yet. We both just stared at each other in disbelief when we read that. I think smelling the horses at the beginning like that eased my nerves a bit. I was getting slightly uncomfortable as we walked through during the tour and after I smelled the horses, I was not afraid anymore. Has anyone ever experienced anything like that before?I wanted to put it in the evidence book that was in the paranormal room, but I had forgotten about it until the next day."

"I noticed a difference in feeling/energy when we went up to the top floor where the drug addicts and alcoholics were housed. The other wards just seemed like empty chaos if that makes any sense, but the top floor felt calm and very sad. I felt really depressed when we sat up there for a while. It was as if maybe the spirits that lingered there were embarrassed and depressed and that is why they would not come out of the rooms for us. We started getting very mild activity from the end of the drug addiction ward. It sounded like possible footsteps. As if, someone was slowly moving around in his or her room. I noticed that the activity started up once we changed the way we spoke to the spirits. It was as if they became more comfortable with us and maybe almost trusted us a little. As soon as others began walking around and making a lot of noise, the activity stopped." Jamie and Denise wrap up their comments with this statement; "In conclusion we know that Trans-Allegheny Lunatic Asylum has had a long history of reported paranormal experiences. The team's experiences in this report bear that out. Our overall conclusion is that the reports of activity are real and verified through our team's investigation."

Just one of many transoms above the doorways at the asylum
Photo by author 2014

Amanda wrote in the evidence book, "While I was walking I heard a woman's voice say *help*." This type of activity can be very unsettling.

Another entry in the evidence book was from a man from Virginia. "While in Ward F, I felt like I was being followed down the hall and in the room where we were told one of the men was smothered, I actually felt something touch my foot." Ward F seems to be on the most active areas noted in the evidence book. The reasoning behind this increase in paranormal activity could simply be due to the violent men who were housed in this area. Ward F was home to some horrific murders and attacks such as the Bedpost Murder. The Bedpost Murder was a violent attack and murder on an innocent patient. The assailaints first tried to hang him. After that failed, they put him on the ground with the leg of a bedpost on his skull. One of the men jumped on the bed causing the leg of the bed to drive into the skull of the victim, killing him.

Other activity in Ward F ranges from being touched to seeing shadows. **Carolina from Virginia** said that she saw a very tall shadow man in Ward F who moved quickly and without sound.

Neal Hammon from Tennessee said, "I heard door slam shut on its own and witnessed many shadows in Ward F." Hair pulling can always be a bit unsettling when it happens in a dark room and you are alone. I've had this happen in a few locations. **Arthur from Maryland** did too. He wrote in the evidence book "While in Ward F the hair on the top of my head top was pulled".

Paul Mihalak ventured to TALA back on July 22 of 2012 with Haunted Heartland Tours as an overnight investigator. He was along with another member of his group from Ohio that evening. He could not wait to explore the building because of the hauntings and all of the stories he had heard. The name of his group is the Hubbard Paranormal Society. As they investigated on their own, they captured shadows in the kitchen area and heard unexplainable noises on the fourth floor of the hospital. They also collected Electronic Voice Phenomena. (EVP's) Paul is a believer of the paranormal after seeing several full body apparitions in his investigations. He considers the fourth floor and the kitchen to be the most active areas as that is where they had their experiences.

Photo by the author 2014

Becky McKinnell came from Ohio and ventured on the overnighter with Haunted Heartland Tours as well. She is a schoolteacher and has always impressed me with her research and knowledge of history. This is Becky's story in her own words.

"Before we were to go to TALA for the overnight investigation, I did some research on the Northern infantry unit that was stationed there during the Civil War. I found that it was the Ohio 7th Infantry and they had the nickname of "Roosters." I also tried to find out who might have died there because there were some reports of someone dying there. I wasn't able to find the name of someone from the 7th that had died there because all the names that I found were mustered out, died in a later battle or died after the war. Jill and I went into the Civil War section of the institution and proceeded to do an EVP session. When we used the term "roosters" and started using some of the names that I had found that were members of the 7th Ohio, we got a definite response for someone. It was a male voice. We were unable to determine the words but the voice sounded excited. Using the dowsing rods, we asked if whom we were talking to knew these men and there was an indication with the rods that it was yes! It was almost as if they were glad to have someone acknowledge them (the ghosts) as real people, not just the typical. ("Is there anyone here?")

The Civil War Section/ Soldiers Home at TALA
Photo by the author 2014

David and Amanda Heath came from Ohio to join us on an overnight event. This is what they had to report after their August 30th overnight at TALA. David shares here story with us; "For the past few years, my wife, Amanda, and I have been enthusiastic about experiencing an overnight paranormal investigation. We have been actively pursuing local venues for novice investigators and recently contacted a veteran paranormal investigator, Sherri Brake. Overall, this was our third ghost hunt after recently exploring the Ohio State Reformatory and the West Virginia Penitentiary."

David continues; "On August 30th 2014, during our first visit to the Trans Alleghany Lunatic Asylum (TALA) in Weston, West Virginia, I had my first paranormal experience, which solidified my belief in apparitions. As a scientist and physician, my initial approach involved a healthy degree of skepticism. After all, my occupation involves accumulating objective data to make clinical decisions. Up to that point, I had adopted a similar approach to the investigation process. In contrast, my wife, a banker by trade, is exceptionally sensitive to paranormal activity and significantly more open minded than I am. I think we complement each other well and represent both perspectives."

"Upon our arrival to TALA, we were taken on a brief tour discussing previous encounters and educating us on the safety while exploring of the faculty. Shortly thereafter, we were released to explore the facility as we saw fit. On the third floor of TAPA, there is an old, unique nursing station. During the days of the active facility, nursing staff actually took up residence within this area and contained bedrooms, closets, bathrooms etc. We hypothesized the area might be more active with my presence since I am a fellow healthcare professional. Around midnight, Amanda and I made our way to the third floor to the nursing quarters. After a brief exploration of the area, I stepped into one of the large bathrooms and began asking some generalized questions. A few minutes passed without any response so I decided to take a photograph into the mirror. I raised both my arms, snap a quick photograph and lowered my arms to my sides. About 10 seconds later, I suddenly felt a distinctive somewhat firm, stroking touch of a hand across the back of my neck. Immediately, beginning from the tip of my nose, tingling and goose bumps spread downward to the tips of my fingers and toes. It felt like lighting shooting out of the tips of my extremities. It was difficult to remain calm so I dashed out of the bathroom and told Amanda what I had felt. Reluctantly, I decided to take a second photo in the mirror and had the exact same experience! There was a second episode of touching to the back of my neck so I told my wife, "I'm out of here!" We continued to explore TALA for the next few hours."

"The feeling of anxiousness stayed with me throughout the night. Around 2 am, although reluctant, Amanda convinced me to return to the nursing quarter's bathroom to take a second look. During this second visit to the nursing quarters, Amanda videotaped me while I took a second photograph in the mirror. Although I did not experience any touching, the video clearly shows a well-formed orb emerging from the bottom of the screen takes a 90-degree right turn then quickly exits the right side of the screen. Although we never visualized an apparition at TALA, we left the facility with a humble appreciation for the deceased. In summary, I still consider myself a scientist who attempts to obtain objective data. However, our experience defies logic and has given me courage to take the step toward belief in the paranormal."

Lois Miller is an investigator who hails from Virginia. She decided to sign up on an overnight ghost hunt after seeing the building featured on one of the popular ghost shows on television. Lois showed up in full ghost hunt attire. She was carrying two gear boxes filled with various investigation gear and had a stash of energy drinks to boot. She had never been on a ghost hunt with me before and this was her first time visiting TALA. She was not to be disappointed, as she would soon find out. A few days after the investigation, I got a rather long email from her. "The entire night I felt as if someone was watching me. I was not hesitant about coming to this ghost hunt solo. I like to work alone when I investigate so that does not bother me at all. I was outside putting some t-shirts that I had bought into my trunk. The back of my shirt pulled away from my skin and was tugged. I turned around to see who was trying to freak me out, and of course, there was no one there. That was early on in the evening. Later on, I would say around 3am, I was sitting in one of the patient rooms on the first floor and I felt an icy coldness around me. Instantly the hairs on my arm stood up. I turned on my digital recorder and tried to capture some voices. All I got was a "sighhhhhhh". It sounded like a man though. I sat there for a while longer. The coldness was around me for about 30 seconds and then dissipated." Lois promised me she would return and planned on spending some more time in that patient's room.

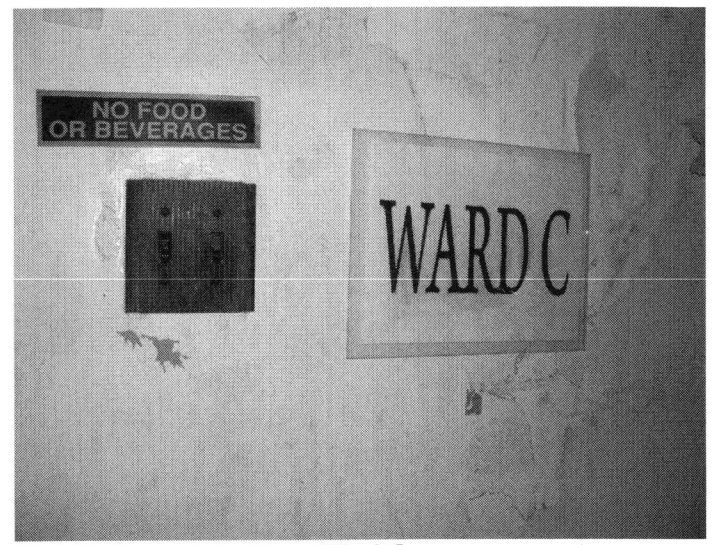

Ward C
Photo by the author

Ray Frady is a team member of the paranormal group, Talkington Paranormal. Ed Talkington was also along for the investigation that evening in 2009 when they toured TALA and readied themselves for the night. Ray told me that he had wanted to see TALA ever since he saw it on a television show. This is his story in his own words:

"In a big room with lots of windows on the very top floor I heard a woman singing in my left ear the song, Frere Jacques. I was alone sitting in a windowsill and it startled me. I whipped my flashlight around and nothing was there. I told a guide later that night what had happened and the guide said that another group had picked up an EVP in the same room of a woman speaking French. In another room, we were sitting in the dark and I could see out in the hallway from where I was sitting. A small white ball of light came out of the ceiling and came down a few feet and turned and went back up through the ceiling. It was very small, almost like a firefly except white. It cast no shadows. In one of the dorms, I asked someone to move a closet door and it moved all by itself. In another area of the building where they have the isolation cells, I never picked up any evidence but that section had a suffocating feel to it. One area in the shower room, it took me three or four attempts to enter the section. I had a heavy feeling, almost suffocating that I wasn't wanted there. Then I finally went in again and the feeling was totally gone." Ray is a believer in the paranormal.

Patient bathrooms. Photo by author 2014

Aaron hails from Ohio and has visited TALA on a few occasions. He has spent the entire night there on several events. This is an account of one of his visits there:

"Investigating the main building of the Trans-Allegheny Lunatic Asylum, I experienced two distinct shadow masses. The first was when I was on the second floor of the asylum, when I reached the end of a long, dark corridor by a utilities room, this "shadow" thing flashed right in front of my face. It was solid and the movement of it was dimensional, and free and independent from the other shadows that moved across the wall from my headlamp. It was too big to be one of the bats that fly through the hallways of the asylum. I got the impression that something was hiding there at the end of that hall and when I got too close, it got up and left. The other shadow mass I encountered was on my next visit to the asylum (both visits were in 2011), and was up on the fourth floor at the time. I was talking to two other people there, and we walked by a room with an open door. I happened to turn my head and look into the room while still talking, and I locked my eyes on a SOLID black shadow form that was also seemingly looking out at me. It was darker than the darkness, and I was shining my headlamp right on it, and the light did NOT illuminate this object, it seemingly "absorbed" the light. As soon as it saw me see it, it ducked behind doorway in the room with lightning-fast speed. The entire event probably lasted less than one second, but I was able to make out a "head", and the rest of the body was a nebulous amoebic mass. The way it moved was like a human, only FASTER! It stood about three feet high, at about half the size of the doorway. It was too big to be a raccoon, possum, or any other type of critter. I was the only one to see this thing, the other two people I was talking with at the time were looking directly down the hall, but as soon as I saw it, I reacted. We went into the room a second or two after I saw it, and there was nothing there but an empty room, the only door in the room was a closet that was wide open with nothing inside and the window was shut and locked. If it was something like an animal, it would still be in there, there was nowhere for ANYTHING to go...and I may have captured these shadows on film, as some of my pictures have unexplained shadow anomalies in them in one of the rooms on the 4th floor."

Aaron continues on "I also got high EMF readings on the third floor consistently in and around this one room halfway down the ward. If I moved a few feet down either direction of the ward, it would immediately dissipate, but as soon as I got near the room again, I would pick up the EMF spikes again...I tested any potential electrical outlets and fixtures for a possible misread, and I could not pinpoint a source. Correspondingly, the readings seemed to be interactive and when I asked it to go up, it would go up, when I asked it to go down, it would go down. It left me at a total loss of understanding."

Aaron visited the asylum on another night in early July of 2011 and while reviewing his tapes a month later, made a discovery. "I was going over my tapes from TALA in July over the weekend and I made a startling discovery on one of them. I was upstairs on one of the wards, I cannot remember which one, but I felt very threatened as if I should leave and I did. But then I challenged myself towards the end of the evening to go back up there and I did. I was hearing a lot of noises like footsteps and shuffling around in a number if the vacant rooms. That's the area where they have a bunch of the rooms cordoned off from the public because the floorboards are all rotted and unsteady, so obviously nobody could be there walking around! Amway, at one point I called out "Is somebody there?' and then there's a few seconds of silence and then I hear a LOUD female cry or moan and nobody was up there with me at the time. I verified this because I walked back down the corridor the way that I had come and whenever I passed a group of people, you could hear then talking as I passed on the tape and there is absolute silence as I walked out the door. It seems to be the loudest EVP I have ever captured. I'm surprised I did not discover it before but I didn't pay that much attention to that segment of the tape. My EMF meter had gone flat by then after spiking off the charts in Ward B."

One of the many hallways at the asylum
Photo by the author 2012

MD Paranormal consisting of Coleman Brumley and Eric Morris investigated TALA and this is what they had to say; During our investigation of the Trans Allegheny Lunatic Asylum this past summer, as we got to the last floor, the 4th, our guide had recommended we just sit quietly and we would most likely hear a lot of disembodied voices and strange noises.

After walking the entire floor, we decided to follow the advice and we sat on the floor of a long hallway with nothing but our digital audio recorders, just allowing our eyes to adjust to the darkness and listening for any sounds. At the end of the hallway was the door to the central stairs, which was allowing just a faint amount of light through the narrow window. Looking down the hall, we kept seeing a shadow covering the window in the door. We knew it was nobody in the hallway as we were the only two on this floor at the time. Our guide had taken a break and left the floor entirely.

I could not believe what I saw next. I saw a creeper shadow figure come out of a red door on the right side of the hall and crawl towards us and across the hall into a door on the left. We then went to take a closer look at the room where the creeper appeared from. We discovered the door was blocked by another door lying on its side, making it very difficult for an animal to emerge from the room. We looked into the room where I saw it enter and we found nothing there either. At this point, I seriously doubted what I just saw and even came to the decision that it was my eyes playing tricks on me as it was approaching 4:30 AM.

About 10 minutes later, our guide returned and asked if we had been experiencing anything. We told him about the shadows at the end of the hallway covering the window and asked him if he was in the central stairway or not, which he said no as he was outside the entire time until he just returned. He then proceeded to tell us what another guide had experienced on this floor recently. He told us another guide saw a shadow creeper figure appear from the red door just up on the right and craw across the floor towards us into a room on the left. What he just described was exactly what I just saw. This totally gave me validation to what I saw that night and it's something that I will never forget." Their website is www.mdparanormal.com

1st floor common area. Photo by author 2008

Unexplained shadows and mists are seen occasionally at the asylum on late night investigations.
Anonymous photographer

Darrin and Danielle Troyer have both attended many of my Haunted Heartland Tour events over the last 12 years. They have both had several experiences while investigating the asylum, even on the daytime tour! This one occurred several years ago and is told to me by Danielle; "A group of us were in Lilly's room where it was filled with toys and balls. At one time, the ball in the middle of the room started moving but was resolved after seeing a window open with the breeze blowing through the room. We still had wishful thinking at this point. We had our recorders turned on and began asking Lilly questions. Not much was going on at this point. An older gentleman was in the room with us and he was asking questions as well. He had some candy that he left on one of the windowsills and told Lilly that he was leaving her some candy since she did not want to talk with us. At this time, I walked to the door and headed out of the room. There were about five to six men left in the room and no women. As I walked out, a voice from the room said "haaa haaa" and it was a young and taunting voice. Of course, I stopped and turned around and everyone in the room had a stunned expression on their faces. Actually to hear a voice with our own ears versus using a digital recorder was classic. To this day, it's one of the best voices I've heard." Danielle continues with her details of the night; "Darren, Randy and Nancy Whitaker and I took a day tour of TALA so we could learn more of the history and see the building before the ghost town later that night. As we entered the building, the tour began on the first floor, left side of the wing.(SOUTH WING) as we began walking and listening to our guide (she was an older woman that had worked there years ago, very knowledgeable and still volunteers there I believe) I noticed that Darren was no longer beside me. I turned around and he was several feet back from me, frozen. He was near the sitting area that they have on the floors. His face was red, and I could tell he was crying. I took to be sweat, and thought that maybe he was having a heart attack. I ran over to him and got my phone, ready to call 911. He shook his head, began to explain to us that he felt something go from the top of his head to his feet and then leave him and it left him with a great feeling of sorrow and pain. Whatever it was, he had felt their pain. This was the first time something like that had ever happened to him. That night, every time we were in that part of the building, it hit him repeatedly. Sometimes bad, sometimes not as bad. There was definitely something there that was communicating with him. After the first incident, as we continued on the tour, I had someone breathe into my left ear. It was a warm breath and made my hair move. It whispered "outside". I turned around, ready to smack Darren and there was no one behind me. I literally backed up against the wall as it really knocked me for a loop and that was a first for me. Those were the main things that happened to us on that hunt with you that night. We also had heard a door slam on the third floor behind us as we walked. It was a very active night and we got hooked."

One of the seclusion cells at TALA. Note the drain in the floor.
Photo by author 2014

Cathi Weber is an investigator from Ohio who investigated TALA in March of 2012. She is sensitive with *Haunted Housewives* and has had a few instances of second sight. She came along as part of the group to investigate the asylum. Other locations that she has investigated in the past include the Ohio State Reformatory, Waverly Hills Sanatorium, Madison Seminary, Zoar Village in Ohio, the Queen Mary, and Lemp Mansion. Cathi told me that her main focus is on spirit communication through any means possible such as dowsing rods, voice recorders, spirit box etc.

This is her experience and in her own words; "My first sense of the asylum was different from my initial feelings on any other previous investigation. I can't say I felt afraid during our orientation walk-through, but I was much more apprehensive than I normally am. I felt watched and studied, as if many entities were checking us out as we walked down the hallways and past the open doors. It was an overwhelming experience! My first paranormal encounter was during the walk-through. We were in the Ward 2 men's area listening to the history of the stabbing that took place there, when I felt compelled to turn around and peruse the end of the hallway we had just come up. As I started to study the darkness at the end of the passageway, a tremendously tall and thin shadow figure, which I perceived to be at the very end of the hall (probably about 100 feet from me) slid across the wall at super speed. It was very fast and was darker than the dark but evident in shape and size. The height had to be 9 feet tall. I was surprised and it just so happened that another investigator was watching as well. We both gasped, "Did you see that?" at the same time. It was amazing and like nothing I had seen before."

Cathi continues on, "My second encounter happened in the same hallway during our investigation phase. My teammates, Darla and Theresa, and myself, were the only people present at the time. Darla was standing about 8 feet away for me down the hall shooting video. Theresa was sitting in a chair in the middle of the hall about the same distance away up the hall recording. I was in between them holding a spirit box in one hand and amplifier in the other. As we started our questioning, I started to fill a tickling on my neck. My first thought was that I was caught on a web or a string and it was brushing back and forth across my neck. I started fidgeting but didn't have a free hand. Darla saw me shrugging my shoulders and asked if I was okay. I said, no, there is something on my neck and it's crawling on my shoulders. I didn't know if perhaps a spider was crawling on me or in my shirt in the back, but that was the sense. Darla came over because by then I was sure a huge bug was inside my shirt. She started brushing my neckline and checking my shirt. Theresa got up and came over to help. I said be sure it didn't crawl inside my shirt. Theresa folded my collar down in the back and started to check with the flashlight. That was when I started to feel a burning on my neck. We were all shocked to discover I had several huge scratch marks going down my back from the top of my right shoulder to almost the middle of my back. That was the first time I had been touched by something unseen in a way that caused me pain. It burned for quite a while but disappeared without incident. I guess you could say TALA left a lasting impression on me!"

Cathi told me in her interview about her belief in the paranormal. She said, "I am skeptical in the sense that I don't believe everything said to be haunted is haunted, and I don't think that every unexplained sound, shadow or movement, or noise is a ghost. But I do firmly believe that something unexplainable is happening around us all the time. There is definitely another side, a spiritual realm that can be experienced if you are open to the possibility."

Lisa visited the Asylum from Virginia. While she was in the Civil War section, she saw a ball move around on the floor in the bathroom across from the nurse's station. Lisa had her pant leg pulled while she was standing in the middle of the room.

Tyfanni has been on several investigations with Haunted Heartland Tours but I would wager to say that TALA is one of her favorites. She shared this with me regarding some of the activity that occurred on a past hunt. "I just wanted to say thank you for the opportunity to investigate TALA with your group. It was truly awesome. My family lives in West Virginia and I have passed by TALA probably fifty times in my adult life, each time looking at it and wishing I could check it out. I have not gotten through my photos from the hunt yet, but I started listening to my audio. My first recording, where I had walked in on a group doing a flashlight session in the children's ward, I got something that literally made me go "holy shit!" During the session, the guy who was asking questions was talking. Over his voice, you hear a male; maybe around 20 years old say, "Go away. Please leave me alone." I wanted to let you know about this evp. What a great night!" Always good to have Tyfanni at an investigation. She has great energy.

Joseph and Darla came to TALA as well-seasoned investigators. They have their own paranormal group in Florida and had ventured north to West Virginia for a whole weekend of ghost hunting. On Friday night, they did a public ghost hunt at the West Virginia Penitentiary and then on Saturday they did a public ghost hunt at TALA. Talk about a long weekend! This is their story as they submitted it to me. "We had always wanted to investigate TALA. This was a dream trip for us and to do both the West Virginia Pen AND TALA the same weekend? WOW! No words can explain our excitement. TALA was a bit quiet for us. We did capture some EVPs on the second floor. In one of the patient rooms, we got a male voice saying, "Is that you?" On the 4th floor we smelled alcohol. Kind of like stale beer. Some other people had been walking ahead of us so we are not sure if they snuck in some beer or what, but it was an odd, old beer kind of a smell. We saw some interesting shadows, almost child-sized on the first floor. That was about it for our night at TALA. We rather expected a bit more, but we know that with the paranormal, you can get quiet nights too. We will definitely go back one day."

Jack Martine showed up at the asylum on my second overnight investigation. He actually drove it straight from Tennessee and was really pumped up on Red Bull when he approached ne at sign in. He had the typical black attire for an investigation but when he opened up one of his metal equipment cases it was packed….with more Red Bull. I tried to talk him into getting a hotel for the night but he insisted on trying to investigate until about 2am and then said he would head back out on the highway. A few months later, he sent me this email. "I had a blast at TALA. I wanted to let you know that overall, I got about seven Class A EVPS. All were recorded in Ward T and Ward R (those wards houses alcoholics and drug addicts at one time) One of the EVPs really caused the hair to stand up on my arms. I had been sitting in Ward T and took out a piece of paper from my notebook. I tore it into a strip and then told whoever was there that I was going to roll a joint. I proceeded to roll the paper up into a Cheech and Chong size joint and then stuck it in my mouth. When reviewing my recordings later on, right after I asked "want to burn one?' you hear a male voice say 'yeeessssss'. Freaked me out!" I hope when Jack shows back up at another hunt as he has promised, he leaves the Red Bull at home and gets a hotel room.

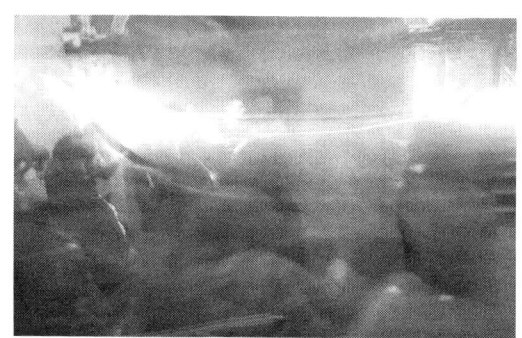

This photo was taken on one of the overnight investigations in 2012. Unusual mist and lights. NO flashlights being used as the lights were still on during the tour. Photo by author

Lisa Roark drove up from Kentucky to stay at TALA for the night. She met up with her West Virginia sister and spent the night together investigating the building. Lisa swears her hair was pulled. She and her sister were walking outside near the old Civil War section and smelled pipe smoke. As Lisa commented about it to her sister Kim, Lisa felt her hair being tugged twice. It was enough to unnerve them both. They did not go back to that section of the asylum all night. I guess that was a little bit more than what they bargained for!

Stephanie came on a public ghost hunt and wrote this in the evidence book; "Late in the night, I heard a loud growl coming from the seclusion rooms."

Marilyn had a few experiences in Ward F. (area where violent males were housed and the bedpost murder was committed) She saw a door move and her shoulder was touched. She said, "I felt very negative in this area."

Pat Harris form Pennsylvania felt a small hand tug at her pants down at the knee area as if a small child was tugging on them. She had been on the first floor and in Lilly's room for a while. She had been singing lullabies. She told me that she felt as if the child did not want her to leave. She felt very sad that night after that experience. Pat told me that the next time she goes back to TALA, she is bringing a doll baby to leave in Lilly's room.

Civil War section fire door

Rodger and Terri came along on one of the Haunted Heartland Tour events in 2012. Roger stands about six foot five and is a well-seasoned Civil War re-enactor. He loves 19th century history and knows his stuff when it comes to all things *War Between the States* related. Roger is a Confederate re-enactor along with his wife Terri. He ended up having an experience with "someone" in the oldest part of the asylum, the Civil War Section, of course!

*Photo in the room where a large cold spot was felt on a
warm summer night. Photo by author 2012*

I get to investigate on my overnight tours as well. What a job perk. I was wandering through the third and fourth floor and I stepped into this one vacant room. Actually I felt drawn into it. It was a very hot humid night and everyone was drenched in sweat. I looked into the darkened shadows with my flashlight and then walked towards the window to look outside. Just as I passed by the seating arrangement, the air stood up on both of my arms. I felt the temperature drop about 10 degrees, maybe more. I did not have a non-contact thermometer on me but I did have my camera. Nothing appeared in my rapid succession of photos but the coldness lasted about thirty seconds. As usual, I wasn't completely prepared for this paranormal experience. Some would argue that this is not paranormal. Remember 'paranormal' is just something that is simply not normal!

14
The Cemeteries
Go Rest High On That Mountain

Although your work on earth is done
Your life in heaven has just begun.
Your struggles here were hard and long
But they're over now, you're finally home

To be laid to rest in peace. It conjures up mental imagery of manicured lawns, nicely decorated headstones and beautiful flowers. This is not always the case in most institution burial grounds. Neglect can be prevalent, not due to uncaring but more due to the lack of funds for upkeep, I imagine. I have seen prison cemeteries with waist high weeds and metal markers for headstones bearing only the inmates name and death date. At Weston, the case is pretty much the same except no markers can be found save but for a few.

Patients who died at the asylum sometimes stayed there. Perhaps I should rephrase that and say that their bodies stayed. Many patients simply had no living relatives to claim them or if they did have family they were either too ashamed to come forward or lived too far away. It would be difficult to travel to Weston to retrieve their remains for burial near the family home, especially back before motorized travel. On occasion, a traveling hobo or transient worker would be committed, sometimes just for public drunkenness, and he would never leave. The asylum provided burial with a minimum of ceremony and display, though there are accounts of doctors and staff attending services.

During the Influenza Epidemic of 1918-1919, it is estimated that 20-40 million people perished worldwide. It left its mark on Weston. This influenza was highly contagious and killed without regard to race, sex, age, wealth or occupation. This virus attacked the respiratory system with a vengeance. When an infected person coughs, sneezes or talks, respiratory droplets are generated and transmitted into the air, and can then can be inhaled by anyone nearby. Additionally, a person who touches something with the virus on it and then touches his or her mouth, eyes or nose can become infected. Imagine the crowded, close conditions within the asylum and you realize it was a recipe for readily transmitted diseases.

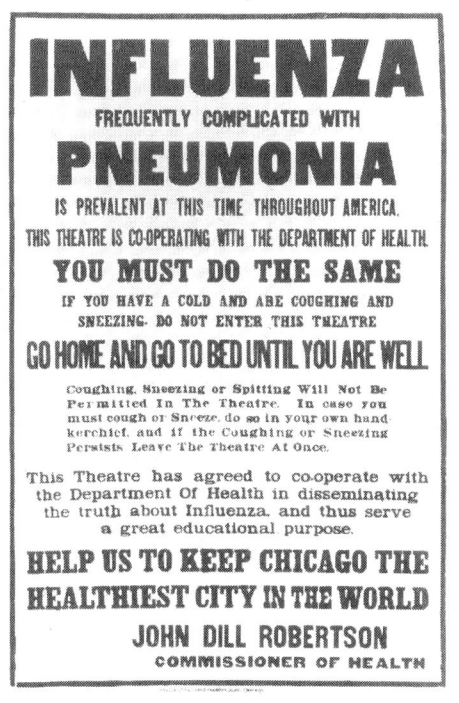

A common poster circulated in many communities. This one was from Chicago

The Public Health Service did not require any states to report influenza before September 27 of 1918. West Virginia first reported the presence of influenza on September 27th, but by that date, the disease was probably present in the state much earlier. Many areas of the state were remote and rural with only a slight scattering of large cities.

Movie theaters were closed, church services cancelled and sales prohibited at the stores. Officials in some communities imposed quarantines. People were advised to avoid shaking hands and to stay indoors, libraries put a halt on lending books and regulations were passed banning spitting. There is little evidence to indicate that these measures were successful in preventing introduction or spread of the disease.

Office of the Public Health Service- photo credit

Across the state, fear was setting in and with good cause. West Virginia University was closed during the epidemic and a fraternity house on campus was turned into an emergency hospital. In Morgantown, theaters and churches were closed and public meetings banned. Closure of schools and prohibition of public gatherings likewise were of doubtful value. The use of facemasks to protect the wearer against infection had its advocates but the poor and rural located had had no means to get access to them. In the asylum, close quarters worked against your chances of not contracting the influenza. The disease hit coal-mining areas harder than other regions. By October, so many West Virginians were either ill themselves or caring for those suffering from the influenza, that a local committee estimated that only 20% of people were able to attend to their jobs outside of the home. Only two mail carriers, for example, were available in Martinsburg to sort and pass out the mail. Gravediggers and undertakers also found themselves overwhelmed with the demand for graves and proper burial. For several weeks in major cities in the state, gravediggers found themselves facing a backload of at least two dozen graves, which needed to be dug by hand each day.

The Haunted History of the Trans Allegheny Lunatic Asylum

Looking thru what burial records are available for the asylum provides you an assortment of various causes of death. Everything from Apoplexy, tuberculosis, breast cancer, gangrene paresis, syphilis and exhaustions is listed. Suicides are noted such as Peter Morris on November 12 of 1892 who used a rope to shorten his life. Gunther Scnell took his own life on August 21 of 1891 by strangulation, probably a rope, belt or sheet but no additional information is given.

Diseases and conditions of the heart and circulatory system such as heart disease and failure, arterial sclerosis, thrombosis, cerebral hemorrhage and myocarditis. Conditions such as epilepsy, bronchitis, pneumonia, dysentery,

Plain old age factored into to death with causes listed as dementia, terminal dementia senility and senile dementia. William Black just died for 'old age' on March 23 1890 at the age of sixty-nine and an even older Pricilla Carter, age ninety-seven in 1907 who also succumbed to 'old age'.

The influenza epidemic claimed asylum patients such as John Murriskc. His cause of death was listed as influenza with his date of death as October 28 1918.Other causes of death listed typical of an asylum were psychosis, manic depression, Paralysis of insane and mental defectives.

Cancer is listed as the cause of death and is repeated often in the records with various types noted such as; pancreas, bladder, renal, stomach and even lip cancer.

Unusual deaths noted were those of Mike Parfeniewtz on April 16 1938 and his thirstiness for lye. Elvira Shaw perished when she had a "cutter accident" on Dec 21 of 1960. She was eighty- six when death knocked on her door. Neville Spinks simply fell out of bed and died on July 17 of 1957.

Surely, there are no sadder deaths than those of babies and children. Stillborn was listed as the cause of death for a few souls such as little baby

Crookshanks who went to Heaven on November 30 of 1958. Baby boy Westfall was a difficult delivery and on July 29 of 1911. African-American Alex Bell died from an epileptic seizure at the young age of eleven on December 9 1918. He was single and eight four years old. Junior Campbell was only nine years old when he passed away from mitral valve issues. Baby girl Perry did not have a much of a chance on December 22 1934. Her cause of death, just a few days from Christmas, was listed as 'died at birth, cord severed'.

Off in the distance is one of three asylum cemeteries
Photo by author 2014

The above named patients were all buried in one of the three cemeteries that were used for asylum burials. Family had not claimed them, had no family or other situations warranted they be interred where they were.
There are less than twenty-five marked graves bearing headstones. I walked one of the state owned cemeteries on a hot August day and while stepping gingerly through thigh high weeds and swatting at bugs, I walked and wondered. I had been told that some of the burials were 3-4 people stacked on top of each other. One cemetery caretaker I know, referred to burials like this as 'double deckers' except these had perhaps three or four. The double decker styles allowed more bodies to be buried and would be thought of as being cost and time effective . It is also the solution to a cemetery with a shortage of space. "Shortage of space?" I thought as I

looked around me. You couldn't see any houses from where I stood. Just meadow grass, woods and a cell phone tower standing guard stoically on a nearby hilltop. I thought of a few fitting lines of prose I knew by heart, as I stood there in the middle of a cemetery filled with thousands, but with only two markers that I could see.

"For those whose names can no longer be read or whose stones have been lost to time, though their names are lost they are loved and will not be forgotten."

It is said that approximately 20,000 people died here between 1864 and the closing in 1994. Some sources state the number as much higher. As I strolled into the first cemetery, I saw a nice marker noting the cemetery. I knew that since many of these bodies were wards of the state, that an elaborate funeral and fancy coffin was highly unlikely. I have been to cemeteries like this before and realized that the dead were probably

Photo by the author 2014

wrapped in blankets or placed in simple pine boxes. As I looked about the cemetery, I began to walk toward the one and only marker I could truly see in the knee-high grass. It said Hermann Emsheimer. After doing a bit of research I found a record for him. He passed away from senile dementia and was a single man of about seventy-five years of age.

Photo by the author 2014

The bugs were beginning to bite a little more ravenously so I moved quickly to the next marker that I could see poking above the tall grass. George Richmond, a married man had died on Valentine's Day 1920. Cause of death, septicemia. This is an infectious blood disease, which can be very serious. It is a life-threatening infection that gets worse very quickly and death can come if it is not treated. He was sixty-four years old. I wondered about his wife. There was a Louise Richmond listed in the burial records and she was six years younger so she *possibly* could have been his wife or maybe a relation. Was she a patient too? Did she have him committed? Who placed his marker? Did his grandchildren know he was here? I always have more questions than answers, it seems. Heading over to the last marker I could find was not an easy task. It was 90 degrees that day and I had on 2 1/2 inch heels and a silk shirt. I was *not* prepared!

*Marker for George Richmond, a faithful servant.
Photo by author 2104*

*Grave of Sallie Fletcher standing solo
Photo by author 2014*

Close up of Sallie's marker photo by author 2014

Sallie Esta Fletcher's marker was small and short. As I squatted down to pull the grass back and read the words, I made a note to find out her story of I could. Researching her name later, I found that she had died from tuberculosis in 1920. A married woman, only thirty years old and with a single marker in a field of tall grass. Next time I visit, I will be sure to bring some flowers for Sallie. It's odd how you get attached to people, especially those you have never met. I was off to the next marker in my first cemetery. It was a good walk and I was glad the sun was beginning to slip down into the horizon. I bent over at the next grave and pulled back some tall grass. I had a hard time pronouncing this person's name. I figured I would probably not be able to find any information on him...or her. I wasn't even sure what the name could possible translate into.

Photo by the author 2014

Imagine my surprise of finding HIM in the burial records. He was listed as Jake Celli! Jake died May 11 of 1925 of paresis, which causes paralysis of limbs and even your eyes. What a horrifying condition. He was fifty-seven years old. What did the 'Fu Carlo' mean? All I could come up with in the translation form Italian to English was this "was Charles". Now that is a bit of a mystery. Was Charles his real name and he went by Jake? In addition, I wondered about the recessed area on his stone. Surely, it has held his photo at one time. What became of it? Did his family have it? Did they know it was gone? I took some notes. Shot some more photographs, stood on the hill, and thought somber thoughts. This was a peaceful location. A bit remote, but peaceful. I was hoping everyone was resting peacefully but the paranormal investigator in me was whispering, "They don't have marked graves and *unmarked* graves can mean unrest in the spirit world."
I hoped this was an exception.

The cemetery as it looked that day in August 2014
Photo by author

In my research, I learned that when the Department of Health and Welfare took over the cemeteries, the markers were removed from the graves. WHAT? This explained a great deal to me. The graves *had* been marked at one time but for efficiency in mowing, they were pulled up and tossed to the side of the cemetery. It was done in 1994 according to

Edward S. Gleason's excellent book *Lunatic, the Rise and Fall of an America Asylum*. I highly recommend his book.

As I walked to the next cemetery, I knew I would find just one grave. It would be that of Jasper Wyatt, a civil war soldier who died in the winter of 1887. He suffered from senile dementia and his grave is marked with his service record in the 6th West Virginia Infantry. His unit saw some action but no large battles. The 6th West Virginia had mustered into service on August 13, 1861, at various locations such as Grafton, Cairo, Parkersburg and Wheeling. The unit spent most of its time defending the B & O Railroad line against southern attacks. The regimental history stated that they mustered out of Federal service on June 10, 1865. Jasper died twenty-two years later and I wondered if post-traumatic stress syndrome had plagued him.

One of the original stone markers from the cemetery
This is on display in the museum area
Photo by author 2014

Some original stone markers on display in the museum area at TALA
Photo by the author 2014

When you venture to the TALA to take a day tour or perhaps a night ghost hunt, I encourage you to take time to stroll the museum area on the first floor. Located in one of the rooms (in 2014) is a display of original stone markers from the cemeteries. I am fond of saying every stone has a story to tell. I am sure these would love for their story to be told. I left TALA a bit sad that afternoon. I was sad for the thousands who are buried with no marker of identification. I took comfort in the fact that I had been told that each of the dead were buried with small glass vial containing their name. I hope one day their names and exact burial location can be found in a non-invasive way. One can only hope.

15
Various Photographs of the Asylum & Grounds

The following pages of photographs were talken during the period of 2008-2014. This book has been my meager attempt at recording some history of one the most impressive buildings I have ever investigated. As a paranormal researcher, a former hospital employee, and a history lover, I have a vast appreciation for all aspects of this asylum. I appreciate the architecture and I relish the Civil War history. I admire Kirkbride's vision as I delved into the history of psychiatry and I was shocked by the barbaric treatments. While walking the burial ground of unclaimed bodies, I found greater respect for those souls. I immersed myself in the world of asylums during this project and was lucky to walk out of the gates unscathed. I saw the darker side of society as I read about primitive America and its fear of lunatics. In regard to the paranormal activity, it continues to fascinate and intrigue me and probably always will. Too many people have had experiences to discount their experiences.

Many past employees, paranormal investigators, and present and past tour guides have shared stories of experiences with me. I appreciated them all and hope that I have collected a few within the pages of this book that have interested you. I realize there is controversy with a subject as sensitive as an asylum and its inhabitants. The patients and families suffered and I do not take this lightly. In my own way, I hope that I have been able to blend the history…and the hauntings into something that will be educational, enlightening, and interesting.

TALA'S OFFICIAL WEBSITE
www.trans-alleghenylunaticasylum.com

Photo by author 2008

Looking at the north side of the main hospital building photo by author 2008

Museum area 2012

Upper floor apartments
Photo by author 2012

Photo by author 2010

Main lobby area 2010 photo by author

*My son, Mason Recco, acting silly with an orb by his side in main lobby
Photo by author 2012*

The asylums old root cellar photo by author 2014

The Greenhouse photo by author 2014

TB Unit porch areas 2014

*The West Fork of the Monongahela River flows in front of the asylum
Photo by author 2013*

Forensics building 2014

*The Medical Center was the hospital's hospital.
The morgue was located here in this 1930s building. Photo by author 2014*

The Haunted History of the Trans Allegheny Lunatic Asylum

Dogwood flower representing the flower of Virginia

Stonemasons carved unusual faces, some scary. Symbolism of frightening figures was believed to scare away evil spirits. They were carved on the exterior of buildings. (near Civil War section) 2014 photo by author

My daughter, Sage Recco. She stands guard in the Civil War section 2014

The entrance to one of the asylum cemeteries
Photo by author 2014

*The Morgue Area
First floor Medical Center building
Photo by author 2014*

The Westoneer
VOL. 3 NO. 4
Mother's Day
WEST VIRGINIA CENTENNIAL, 1963

Published By
WESTON STATE HOSPITAL Weston, W.Va.

Weston Hospital 1992

ABOUT THE AUTHOR

Sherri Brake is an author, paranormal researcher, and a para-historian. Sherri has investigated the paranormal since the early 1980s and developed her own successful haunted tour company in 2003. She shares her love of dark history with thousands of guests yearly. She is a popular guest on radio, and has appeared on various documentaries and shows on PBS, SYFY, and the Discovery channel. Brake enjoys hosting her tours, events, and instructing paranormal classes. As a civil war re enactor, Sherri enjoys history of the 19th century, both military and civilian.

The author lives in central West Virginia with her husband on a 100-acre farm. She is the proud mother of two adult children who are not afraid of the dark or old creepy buildings. You may email her at SherriBrake@gmail.com
Visit her website at www.HauntedHistory.net

BIBLIOGRAPHY

"Sixth Annual Report of the Directors & Superintendent of the West Virginia Hospital for the Insane" 1869, 7-9

Biennial report of Directors, 1878-1880, 15-16.

Scull, Andrew, ed. Madhouses, Mad-Doctors, and Madmen: The Social History of Psychiatry in the Victorian Era. Philadelphia: University of Pennsylvania Press, 1981.

Yanni, Carla. The Architecture of Madness: Insane Asylums in the United States. Minneapolis: University of Minnesota Press, 2007.

"National Register Information System". National Register of Historic Places. National Park Service. 2010.

Swick, Gerald D. "Weston State Hospital". Ken Sullivan (ed.) The West Virginia Encyclopedia. Charleston, W.V.: West Virginia Humanities Council. p. 779 2006.

Stalnaker, Joy Gilchrist, A Short History of
Weston Hospital (Horner, West Virginia: Hacker's Creek, 2001), 3-7

Jacks, Kim Weston State Hospital, Thesis
Submitted to the Eberly College of Arts and Sciences at West Virginia University, Morgantown, WV 2008.

Stowe, Steven M. Doctoring in the South. Chapel Hill: University of North Carolina Press, 2004.

Cook, Roy Bird. "History of Lewis County". 1924.

Preston, R. J. "Some Statistics and Partial History of the Insane in Virginia." American Journal of Insanity" 57, no. 2 October 1900.

Wesley Atkinson George and Alvero Franklin Gibbs,
Prominent Men of West Virginia, Wheeling: W. L. Callin, 1890

Adler, "Yesteryears," Weston Democrat, July 6, 1988, from Weston Democrat, July 10, 1871.

Hills, R., Thomas B. Camden, et. al. Reports of the Directors and Superintendent of the West Virginia Hospital for the Insane. Wheeling and Charleston: Public Printers, 1866, 1869, 1870, 1871, 1872, 1873, 1874, 1875-6, 1877-8, 1879-80, 1881-2, 1885-6, 1891-2, 1893-4, 1895-6, 1897-8, 1899-1900, in entirety or excerpted

Bly, Nellie. Ten Days in a Mad-House. New York: Ian L. Munro, 1887.

Joinson, Carla, "The Perception and Treatment of Insanity in Southern Appalachia" 2012.

"Old Asylums Decay, While Some strive for Restoration". The Baltimore Sun. 2008.

"Cemeteries of Lewis County, W Va and Adjacent Counties Volume XII" complied by Marlene Tenney, Joy Stalnaker and the late Hartzel Strader. Hackers Creek Pioneer Descendants

"Morgantown Contractor Buys Old Weston State Hospital". Charleston Daily Mail. 2007.

Davis, Jamie with Samuel Queen. Haunted; Asylums, Prisons, and Sanatoriums. Llewellyn 2013.

Historic West Virginia: The National Register of Historic Places. Charleston, W.Va.: West Virginia Division of Culture and History: State Historic Preservation Office. 2000. pp. 74–75

Camden M.D., Thomas Bland. "My Recollections and Experiences of the Civil War. West Virginia" McClain Printing Company, 2000.

Davis, Mark "Voices from the Asylum: West Riding Pauper Lunatic Asylum" Amberley Publishing 2013

Shoerter, Edward. "A History of Psychiatry: From the Era of the Asylum to the Age of Prozac" Wiley 1998.

Porter, Roy. " Madness: A Brief History" Oxford University Press 2003.

Whittaker, Robert. Mad in America: Bad Science, Bad Medicine, and the Enduring Mistreatment of the Mentally Ill Basic Books 2010.

Hoog, Charles Edgar. The West Virginia Blue Book -West Virginia Code Supplement. 1918

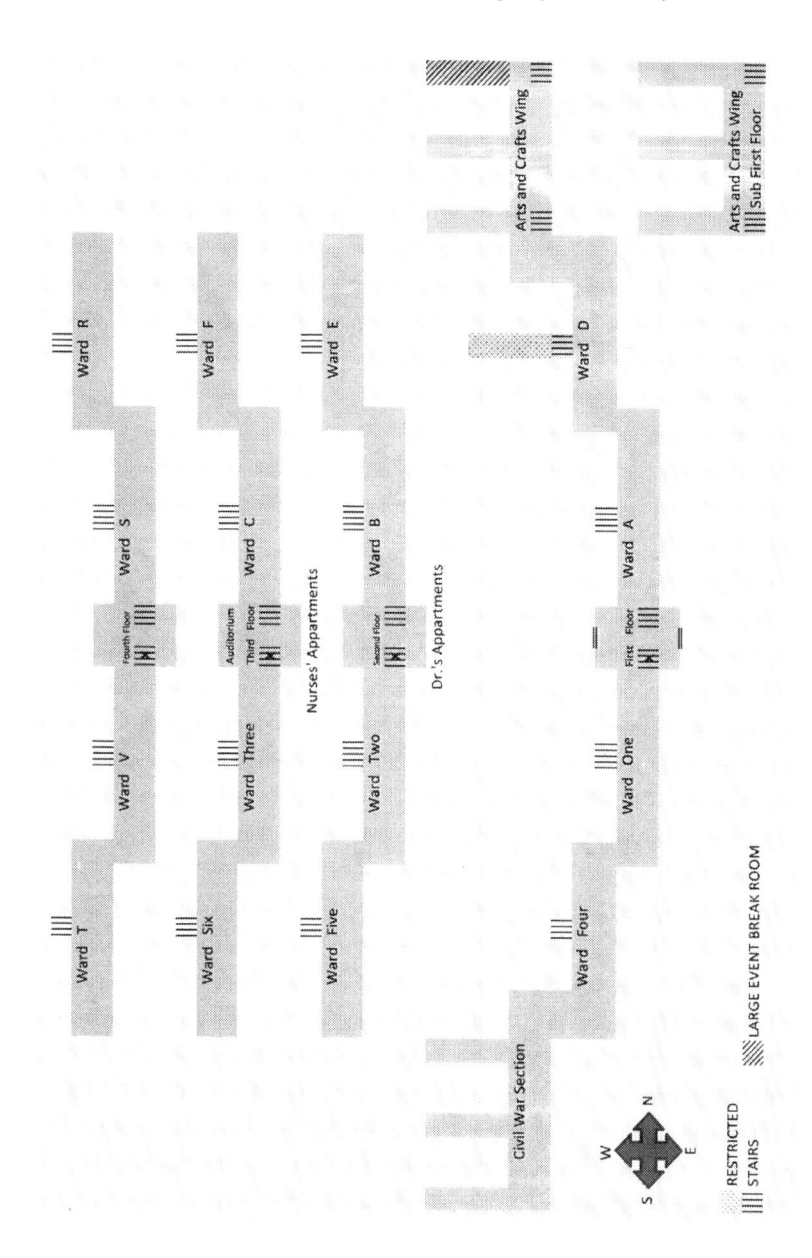

Map supplied by Trans-Allegheny Lunatic Asylum

Notes

Made in the USA
Lexington, KY
14 December 2019